To Mosaba
This is th[e]
I wrat

Best Wish[es]
John H[...]

ROTHERY ON COLLECTING

ROTHERY ON COLLECTING

John Rothery

Illustrations by Bryan Martin

The Book Guild Ltd
Sussex, England

First published in Great Britain in 2002 by
The Book Guild Ltd
25 High Street,
Lewes, East Sussex
BN7 2LU

Typesetting in Times by
Keyboard Services, Luton, Bedfordshire

Printed in Great Britain by
Bookcraft (Bath) Ltd, Avon

A catalogue record for this book is available from
The British Library

ISBN 1 85776 639 3

This book is dedicated to the memory of the following at whose passing the world became more sad and grey:

Ray Coker
Dave Crabtree
Bertie Curnow
Marcus Dinely
Ronnie Dufty
Tony Earle
Jimmy Goode
Dougie Nie
Hughie Nimmo
Richard Washer

CONTENTS

ACKNOWLEDGEMENTS

May I thank my fellow members of the antique trade who gave freely of their time and were generous with their encouragement.

My customers who for months put up with me trying out various passages of this book on them.

My sincere thanks to Bryan Martin for the cartoons.

Mostly I am forever grateful for the help and encouragement of the lady in my life, Miss Shena Jeannette Lay, who proved yet again to be my best friend by not only ensuring a constant supply of tea but by actually buying me a word processor on which this book was written.

AUTHOR'S NOTE

You know, when asked to write this book, I was really most reluctant to do so for two reasons. Firstly, I cannot for one minute imagine anyone being the slightest bit interested in my opinions on the subject and secondly, having never been a collector, I feel a bit like the Pope on the subject of birth control. If you do not play the game, you should not state the rules.

A lifetime as a professional dealer has however given me a deep insight into the attitudes and behaviour of the average collector and it is with heavy heart that I have watched them blunder from mistake to mistake as they struggle to come to grips with the basic concepts of the art of collecting.

The widely-held misconceptions of most people on the subject are constantly fed by the plethora of rather silly TV programmes currently being shown in which all dealers are portrayed as being devious, cheating villains, old ladies are constantly being swindled and the only knowledgeable, honest brokers are the auctioneers. All of which is, in fact, very far from the truth.

Some of my clients, I am very proud to say, have dealt with me for over 40 years and I now sometimes serve the third generation of collectors whose grandparents I helped to start collecting. This is partly due to the fact that I have always tried to guide people away from the pitfalls and misconceptions, towards a more rewarding and enjoyable approach to the hobby. Not all people have found my advice and guidance welcome and, indeed, some have felt my approach to be somewhat patronising, to the extent that one gentleman told me,

'Mr Rothery, if I had to deal with you, I would give up collecting.' Well, I suppose you can't win them all and the gentleman was entitled to his own opinion.

My main method of getting the finer points of the subject across to people is by the use of illustrative stories or, as one client liked to describe them, 'The parables according to Saint John'. You will find them throughout this book and they do tend to make the points that need to be made. They are, in fact, all true although some have been disguised to save nice people from embarrassment.

Many times when I have been giving advice to my clients, they have commented that, while technical books on antiques abound, there has never been a book of common sense and practical advice on the basic concepts and principles of collecting and why had somebody not written one. It is them that you must thank – or blame!

As my entire career has been in the field of naval and military antiques, I took the trouble to show the drafts of this book to many established dealers in other fields of collecting. They have all assured me that what I have said and the points that I have made are equally relevant to all and every form of collecting. On completion, the final draft was also shown to a wide variety of collectors and other people who are mentioned in the book, to gauge their reactions. Most were fairly predictable.

I was informed by the boot sale brigade and the lower end of the fair and specialist fair operators that, in the event of the book ever getting published, I may expect great physical violence to both myself and my property. This does not bother me greatly but does rather show the type of people that one might expect to meet at these events.

I have further been informed that my presence will not be welcome at some of the auction houses. I think I can live with that. Through friends in the media, I have heard that if the book gathers too much credibility I shall almost certainly be subjected to as much ridicule and vilification as both the TV people and the press can muster.

What is it I wonder that all these people are frightened of? Not one of the people who are less than pleased at what I have said has disputed that my comments are true or honestly held opinions, even if they do not like my phraseology.

Most of the collectors have enjoyed it despite recognising themselves and their little foibles, many have been kind enough to tell me that in their opinion it is a must for anyone who is, or is thinking of, becoming a collector.

The reaction of the legitimate trade surprised me as, to a man, they thanked me and made such comments as 'About time somebody told the truth,' and, 'Thank you Mr Rothery, someone had to tell our side.' A comment was made: 'You don't like collectors very much do you Mr Rothery?' Absolute rubbish, I love the vast majority of collectors dearly and my own in particular. What I do not like are rude, arrogant people, whether they are collectors or not.

'You surprise me Mr Rothery. You and some of your fellow dealers seem to have what I can only describe as disdain for money, which is the opposite of what we are all led to believe.' Not so, we need money to live on and feed our kids just like anyone else. We do however have a deep disdain for greed and greedy people.

Interesting and useful as this feedback was, we must not lose sight of why I wrote this book. I wrote it for you, to help and guide you.

I suggest you read it and digest it then please go out, look, listen and ask questions. Then think hard about what you see and hear and judge its veracity and usefulness for yourself.

GLOSSARY

AFTER   See *attributed to* and *style of*. Usually 'a long time after'.

ATTRIBUTED TO   Auction speak for a lot that might be by a well-known artist or maker. It rarely is. See *after* and *style of*.

AUCTION FEVER   Mild state of madness when a bidder at an auction allows their greed or enthusiasm to get the better of their common sense and continues bidding well beyond the value of the lot.

BLUE RINSE BRIGADE   Ladies who run stalls at antiques markets and fairs. Can sometimes be applied to men. Usually housewives playing at dealers in both cases.

BRAIN PICKER   Pain in the proverbial, constantly asking for information but rarely doing any business. Very often fringe dealer.

BROWSER   See *time-waster*, *looker* etc.

CRAPALATA   Dealer speak for rubbish.

CUSTOMER   Rare and precious breed that buys, sells and exchanges goods. Sadly in danger of extinction. Not to be confused with *looker*, *time-waster* or *brain picker*.

EROTICA   Dirty pictures and objects owned by posh people. See also *pornography*.

EXPERT   Derogatory term for people who think they are. Self-opinionated know-all. Much used by media, not to be taken seriously in this context.

FAIR FANTASIES   Misinformation widely dispensed at antiques and specialist fairs.

GOB ON A STICK Media term for pundits or experts appearing on TV shows.

HENS TEETH, Rare as Description of item that is extremely difficult to find. See also *rocking horse droppings*.

'I'LL TELL HER' Standard lie used by *brain pickers* having obtained information and price of an item which is probably their property but that they are allegedly selling on behalf of a non-existent, elderly relative.

KNOCKER Lowest form of dealer who knocks on doors trying to beg, buy and sometimes steal antiques. Person who constantly finds fault with any item they are shown. Both specimens to be avoided at all costs.

KNOWLEDGEABLE Term of admiration for person who knows what they are talking about. Rarely used. Sometimes prefixed by 'quite' when grudgingly accepting that someone knows a thing or two, i.e. 'She is quite knowledgeable.'

LOOKER Person who spends an inordinate amount of time in shops but rarely, if ever, buys anything. Announces itself with cry of 'just looking' and nervous giggle. Has tendency to look with its fingers.

MALE MODEL, DUSTMAN AND SOLICITOR SYNDROME Used to describe people of any trade or profession who, not satisfied with cocking up their own job, cause mayhem among collectors by claiming to 'know about antiques'.

MIRACLE SEEKER Person who expects to find the impossible at equally impossible prices.

NAGASAKI BUS STOP Unspecified collectors item, a whatsit or thingamabob.

OPTIMIST See miracle seeker.

PORNOGRAPHY Dirty pictures and objects owned by poor people. See also *erotica*.

RIPPED OFF Plaintive cry of smartarse who, having thought they'd got the better of a deal, found out that they had not. Or noun, **RIP OFF**: 'It's a rip off', used to describe reasonable price of an item, which the same smartarse cannot afford.

ROCKING HORSE DROPPINGS, Rare as   Virtually non-existent. See also *hen's teeth*.

SHOP   Establishment where goods are bought, sold and exchanged. Sometimes gives valuations for a small fee. Not to be confused with social services, free advice centre for disadvantaged collectors or adult crèche for husbands while wives go shopping.

SPECULATIVE LOT   Box of rubbish that auction house cannot be bothered to lot up. Often used when they do not know what an item is.

STYLE OF   Auction house speak for obvious copy or fake which vaguely resembles something half decent.

TFI   Initials for 'That flaming idiot', although there is another interpretation. Originally nickname of well-known and thoroughly despised fringe dealer who has the unique distinction of not only doing everything wrong, but steadfastly refusing to either listen or learn. Now generally applied to any collector whose ignorance and bad manners, combined with their dishonesty, put them beyond redemption.

THE STARE   Short form of 'the *Antiques Roadshow* Stare'. Glazed look which appears on the faces of people when they are having their treasures, appraised. While supposedly showing interest, it actually interprets as 'Why doesn't this boring old fart shut up and just tell me what it's worth?'

TIME-WASTER   Person who hangs around shops, wants to handle everything in sight, talks a lot of rubbish and has no intention of buying.

TRADE GROUPIES   Sycophants who hang around the fringe of the trade, claiming to know everybody worth knowing. In extreme cases, have cards printed describing themselves as writers, consultants or even experts. They are usually only these things when not following their normal dead-end job of driving a milk float or being a Member of Parliament.

'Just looking'

XV

1

The Philosophy of Collecting

'I do not like that picture, Jones.'
'You do not live with it, Smith'
'How much did you pay for it?'
'That is no concern of yours.'
'What is it worth?'
'Hours of pleasure every time I look at it.'
'So how do you know that you have not been ripped off?'

'Because I am perfectly happy with it and what I paid for it. I cannot therefore have been ripped off. You see Smith; my philosophy is that in this house this is my behind in my armchair, looking at my collection, paid for with my money. I do not give one jot for the opinions of Messrs Sotheby's, Christies or your friends who think they know about antiques when they are not being male models, dustmen or solicitors.'

Jones is quite right. In his home, he is the sole arbiter of what he is or what he is not going to collect and what he is going to pay for his collection. It is nobody's business but his own.

You may choose in your home to adopt the same approach; many collectors do.

There is, as always, another point of view. Some collectors crave the approbation of their friends and fellow collectors:

'I say what a lovely picture.'

1

'Yes, every one admires it.'

'How much did you pay for it?'

'Five hundred pounds, but I had it looked at by an expert who works with my brother at the local abattoir and he said I should insure it for £700.'

'Gosh! That was a bargain. Aren't you clever?'

This person is equally right. They get immense pleasure and reassurance from the flow of compliments being paid to their good taste and shrewdness, the evidence of which hangs in the hall and is the first thing seen by visiting friends and relatives. To them, this is well worth the £500 they have paid.

One client, with whom I had spent a great deal of time explaining the basics of medal collecting, came into the shop one day in a terrible state. When I asked him what was wrong, he informed me that he had just bought some medals but was dreading going home with them. He knew that when he showed them to his fellow collectors they would tell him that he had bought the wrong thing, as they always did whenever he showed them his latest acquisitions. I tried all sorts of arguments with him but in the end had to tell him, 'Look sir, you have either got to stop bothering about what other people think or give up collecting altogether before it makes you ill.'

Mr Horrocks was a lovely man who, despite his rather limited income, collected coins. Most coin collectors and 'experts' will tell you never to bother with any coins that are not in 'very fine' or 'uncirculated' condition, but not our Mr Horrocks. Completely disregarding all the usual grading of coins, he would arrive at the shop: 'Morning Rothery, have you got a Queen Anne crown in "affordable" condition?' His feeling was that, rough as the condition might be, it was still a Queen Anne crown.

Mr G had the same philosophy with medals. Unlike most medal collectors, who will not accept a medal at any price if the naming has been tampered with, he told me on many occasions, 'Look Mr Rothery, that is a perfectly genuine medal.

The fact that the name has been altered only means to me that I can afford it.'

On one occasion I was in a shop with a lady who was a well-known collector of miniature portraits. The proprietor, with great pride, produced three for her consideration. He explained to her that this one was by Holbein, the famous 16th-century miniaturist, the next by a not so famous artist but a bargain as he was only asking half what one by the same artist had made recently in auction, and the third was of a famous historical figure with a very comprehensive history of that person and an impeccable family provenance. After a cursory examination the lady very graciously rejected all three. The dealer, rather put out by this rejection, said, 'But madam, surely this is a great opportunity for you to add to your collection not only the work of a great painter but a historically important piece and to acquire a very good bargain.'

'True,' she replied, 'but they are not pretty.' This lady's philosophy was, quite rightly in my opinion, that regardless of any historical or financial considerations the miniatures were not to her liking and she did not want them in her collection.

There are of course those, not real collectors, who would have bought them because they could show off that they had a Holbein or a bargain. Is that collecting or purely an ego trip?

Whilst on the subject of our approach to collecting, let me make mention of a situation that you will find yourself faced with, if indeed it has not already happened. It stands to reason that in whatever field you select, the most common and, therefore, the less expensive items will come fairly quickly and that as you progress new additions will become more difficult to find and more expensive, until eventually new items are not only extremely rare but extremely expensive. When this happens I find that a great many collectors become disillusioned and rather negative: 'There's nothing about that I haven't already got and when it is, it's too expensive. I don't think I'll

3

bother any more.' Some retire the collection to the attic, others sell it. Throughout this book I have said, 'When collecting is no longer fun go and do something else,' but there is a more positive approach to the situation.

We could argue that as the rare items are so costly we need plenty of time to build up our finances between each purchase so that we have the funds to hand for the rare occasions when we do find something. Some might rightly argue that the tougher the hunt gets the more fun it is and the greater the satisfaction when we do find the item of our desire.

One thing that has always confused me is the reluctance of a great many collectors to adopt a second string to their collecting bow. If one is collecting teacups then why not teaspoons? If its bicycles then why not cycling accessories or cycle club trophies? With any collection it is always a good idea to have a good library, so what about collecting old books and catalogues on your pet subject?

Many of my clients who do start a secondary collection seem to think that to do so is some sort of admission of failure. They get rather embarrassed and apologetic: 'I'm afraid, Mr Rothery, I've started to collect a few bits of something else.' It's the ego raising its ugly head again. When this happens I do not see the person as being weak but as someone who has the good sense to recognise the problem and an open enough mind to explore a different path.

My favourite example of the 'free thinker' was in an art gallery. A somewhat pushy young lady, who probably got her MA from Redbrick University last week, was showing around a real old gent of the old school who probably had 50 years of experience. She explained the various pictures to him in the patronising manner that art gallery people adopt, until finally, pointing with his silver-topped cane, the old boy said, 'I'd take that one.' The girl looked aghast. 'But sir, that one is unsigned!' The old boy looked her straight in the eye. 'Young lady, for the past 50 years I have collected art, not autographs.'

4

'They say.'
'What say they?'
'Who be they?'
'I care not what they say.'

I think it was Voltaire who said that, but no doubt someone will put me right if I am mistaken, and therein lies one of the problems. So many self-appointed pundits think they have a God-given right, if not a duty, to tell people what they should or what they should not collect. They have neither right nor duty and my advice is to develop your own philosophy on collecting and, like Voltaire, 'care not what *they* say'.

2

The Knowledge

Many times I am asked, 'How did you come to know all about antiques?'

The answer to that one is I do not know all about antiques. I am still learning. Should you ever have the misfortune to meet anyone who claims to know all about antiques, my advice would be to avoid them like the plague. They are fools and they are dangerous fools.

What little I do know, I have learnt mostly by making mistakes. The Polynesians have a saying, 'The man who has never stumbled, has never walked'. I have my own version: 'Show me the collector who has never made a mistake and I'll show you a liar'.

I find it rather amusing how people will tell you at great length and in even greater detail about the wonderful finds they have made, but never mention the monumental cock-ups that they have made rather more of, and believe me they have made them. So have I and so will you. We must learn to laugh at them and gain knowledge from them.

So where and how do we start?

Books

Books are as good a place as any, books and more books. Big books, little books, cheap books, expensive books, lots and lots of books – read all you can lay your hands on. You need to start building as comprehensive a library as possible on your chosen subject. You will find that you are constantly referring back to one or other of them to check or recheck something that you have seen or acquired.

'Isn't there one definitive book?' I hear the more tight-fisted, sorry, cost-conscious of you cry, 'books are very expensive.' And, indeed, many of them are. But your mistakes could be more expensive and how do you put a price on knowledge?

There have been many attempts at writing 'definitive' books on almost every subject imaginable to do with collecting; usually by those I call 'once only' authors. These are people who have made a lifelong study of a subject but have never written anything in their lives. Egged on by friends and relatives ('You should write a book'), they eventually do, rather as I am doing now!

These books are usually very good indeed being as they are the culmination of a lifelong study. They do tend sometimes to be on a very narrow and specialised field.

Let us take as examples these two:

The Mantons by Keith Neal. This is a superb study of two of England's greatest gun makers, the brothers Joseph and John Manton. It is beautifully illustrated with masses of in-depth information, not only on the works of the brothers, but on their family history; it even lists the patents they took out on their various inventions.

No sooner had the book been published, than a great many people contacted the author all with additional information on the brothers and their products, so much so that Mr Neal very wisely collated this additional information and published *The Supplement to the Mantons*. I would not mind betting that even more information arrived after the supplement was published.

The other example, *The Webley Story*, by a gentleman who regaled in the name of William Chipchase Dowell, was an almost identical situation. Unfortunately, when after the publication of his book the additional information flooded in, Mr Dowell, I am told, took a less robust view and not only gave up writing, but collecting as well.

In both these cases the books were absolutely first class. They were not wrong in any way, but neither was the complete story told. This in no way detracts from their value as an excellent source of reference.

Here is a story which I think illustrates the problems of the knowledgeable author.

A most unusual and beautiful silver-hilted, small sword came my way and, not being too sure of the assay marks, I took it to a highly reputable and respected silversmith. Having looked at it very carefully and checked it against several books, he shook his head in amazement and told me, 'Mr Rothery, I have practised as a silversmith for over 40 years. During this time, I have collected and studied the works of this maker, so much so that I have been the author of countless articles and books on silver in general and this man in particular. This item is, in my opinion, absolutely genuine and one of the finest examples of his work that I have ever seen, but if anyone had asked me had he made sword mountings, I would have said most certainly not.'

My conclusion, dear reader, is not only has there never been a 'definitive' book, but there never will be.

A much-heard comment when really knowledgeable people are gathered together is: 'Are you *sure*, old boy? Well I'm buggered! I never knew that.' A little motto: 'Better the considerations of the expert than the certainty of a fool'.

Moving on to books in general, it was once said that if you copy someone else's book, that is plagiarism, but if you copy a dozen, that is research. Most books on specialised subjects contain very similar information. They often also contain long-held but incorrect theories for no other reason than somebody got it wrong in a book donkeys years ago and these mistakes are repeated over and over again in subsequent books until they become accepted as fact.

Against all this, it is also the case that all books contain some gem of information or a picture that is not in any other book. The interpretation of known information by various authors can also give the researcher a different slant on an item.

When I used to give talks, I would read passages from two particular books, one of which referred to 'the mythical special dagger for the German Navy', the other to 'the non-existent Parker wind-up air pistol', both books apparently suggesting that these items did not exist. At this point I would produce both items.

As I told my audiences at the time, this did not mean that the authors were idiots or the books a load of rubbish, as most of the information contained in them was jolly good stuff. The authors were doing no more than expressing an honestly held opinion based on the information available at the time.

I suppose there must be about a hundred books on and around my desk, backed up by several hundred more in my study at home. Many of these books are in a pretty dire state from constant use. Not a day goes by without one or another of them getting looked at. If, with all my professional experience and knowledge, I still need a good library, it's a pound to a penny that you will.

Remember always with books, even the best are not perfect and while we are happy to be advised and guided by them to help us form our own opinions, they are only printer's ink on paper and not letters of fire on tablets of stone. 'No honestly, I saw it in a book; its absolutely true' is something we have all heard. Let us sincerely hope that people who believe everything they read in a book never lay their hands on a copy of *Mein Kampf*.

There are two types of book which I consider to be quite irrelevant to the serious collector. The coffee-table book, which tends to show the great collections in museums around the world, such as the Fabergé in the Hermitage or royal collections in various palaces. They show lots of fantastic items that we lesser mortals are never likely to have in our collections – not a lot of use to us, nice as they are. The funny thing about these books is that they are always the ones that fond relatives buy us for Christmas and birthdays, so you will probably end up with them anyway.

The other type of book, which is not only irrelevant but also downright dangerous, is the price guide or catalogue. Here are a couple of stories to illustrate the point.

A young aspiring collector has just purchased, at considerable expense, a medals price guide. He is talking to a member of my staff.

'What do you think of the book?'

'Lots of interesting information and very useful for identification.'

'Can I ask you something that puzzles me?'

'Sure, what's your problem?'

'Well, all these medals you have on show, some are half the price this book says they should be, some are a lot more than the book says and you do not have one medal anywhere near what my book says the price should be.'

'Ah, that's easy. What name is on the cover of your book?'

'Spinks.'

'And what name is on our window?'

'Rothery's.'

'Well, Mr Rothery does not tell Mr Spinks what price to charge for medals and Mr Spinks most assuredly does not tell Mr Rothery what prices he should charge.'

A trifle hard on the kid who had spent a lot of money on the book, but of course absolutely true.

Another example of how silly these guides can be was when one of the national papers produced an antiques price guide. This showed a Victorian military badge with a perfectly

10

accurate description of the item, which they valued at £75. It so happened that at the time we had an identical specimen priced at £37.50. Naturally, we put the price guide in the cabinet alongside the badge. This gave cause for much mirth and ribald comment among the regulars and staff until one young man of a more sober frame of mind expressed surprise at the difference and asked why everyone thought it amusing. It had to be pointed out to him that not only was the guide price obviously wrong, but my lower price was apparently equally wrong since even at £37.50 nobody had wanted to buy the badge.

One of the cleverest bits of marketing in recent years has been the proliferation of various so-called annual price guides. These as a rule show every collectable imaginable at extremely high prices at which nobody in their right mind either buys or sells. What happens is that a gullible public rushes home with their latest acquisition and compares what they have just paid with what 'the guide' says. Invariably of course 'the guide' value is much higher, so the purchaser is over the moon at how shrewd and clever he has been. Each year, when the latest guide comes out, they rush to buy it – very good business for the publisher. I wish that I had thought of it first.

Now come on, use your common sense! Dealers can read. Do you honestly think for one minute that hard-nosed professionals would really sell goods at far below their true value?

In my opinion, these so-called guides do no more than boost the ego of rather greedy people who like to think that everything they have bought has been a bargain. Personally I really cannot take price guides seriously and I would advise you to treat them with extreme caution and not consider them a serious part of your library.

Finally, a good book of hallmarks is useful, not only to the gold and silver collector but also to anyone collecting other items which might have gold or silver mounts, such as walking sticks. These books are not expensive and have the added advantage of rarely becoming out of date. Armed with such a book you can of course immediately and accurately date any item which bears the marks.

In the same vein, if you collect anything which might have a family crest on it, such as china or pewter, then you would be well advised to get a good book on heraldry to enable you to identify the previous owners and possibly date the item.

Having built a library, it is amazing how few collectors know how to use it to their best advantage. Please let me guide you away from the dangers of what I call 'shallow knowledge'. That old saying that 'a little knowledge is dangerous' is never truer than in the world of antiques.

So many collectors, especially the one-book variety, will on obtaining an addition to their collection, flick through their book and as soon as they see something vaguely resembling the item to hand assume that that is what they have got. Seldom, if ever, do they read the full description or turn over the page and read about the multitude of varieties and different dates that the item might be. God forbid that they should perhaps check it against a couple of other books and compare the various authors' opinions.

Let us look at this in practice. 'That's a wrong 'un,' announces the office know-all on seeing the rather nice piece of silver you have just acquired. 'The hallmark is 1775, the crest has been added later and the inscription is 1865.' He is, of course, partly right. The piece was made in 1775 as the assay marks show, and the crest was obviously added later. Could this be due to the fact that the original owner was not granted their arms until a later date and then had all the family silver engraved at the same time? It was at one time very common for people to make gifts or present trophies from their family silver and to have them suitably inscribed to fit the occasion. In the early days, I was always buying shooting cups and rose bowls with a similar background which I would present to the various clubs who had asked me if I would put up a prize for something or another. I suppose in years to come someone might comment on a 1775 silver rose bowl with a later crest of Lord Muckpiddle and an inscription along the lines of 'Presented to the best recruit, Muckpiddle Volunteers 1865' and a further inscription, 'Schools debating prize presented by John Rothery 1973'.

A purist, I suppose, would see the item as a nice 1775 rose bowl ruined by later additions. The office expert would declare it 'a wrong 'un', but I would like to think that a real collector with a decent library containing perhaps some of the books that I have recommended would research the date and maker, the crest of Lord Muckpiddle, the history of the Muckpiddle volunteers and see it as a far more interesting piece than a plain rose bowl, most certainly not 'a wrong 'un' and 'Can you imagine, its the one old man Rothery mentions in his book on collecting!'

Before leaving books, please remember the old adage about judging books by their covers. If you see any title that might in the slightest way contain information on your chosen subject, then you would do well to check it very carefully before dismissing it as an addition to your library. I well recall a particularly horrid little book that I was about to discard because of its title (*The Gun Dealer's Handbook*) when, for some unknown reason, I looked through it. While it purported to be about guns, I was astonished to find in it a chapter on Japanese swords, which I think was the best thing I had ever seen as a primer on the subject. Another chapter was about the engraving of the blades of Bowie knives with anti-slavery propaganda, an aspect of blade engraving which up to that time I had never heard of.

On the subject of Bowie knives and to illustrate much of what I have said about books and the collector, one final story.

Many years ago, there was a lovely guy by the name of Richard Washer, who always hung around on the fringe of the trade playing at the big dealer. Richard was always about to pull off the deal of the century but invariably needed a pee when it was his round! Not for nothing was he known as 'Tricky Dickie' and any item he had on offer was treated with the greatest of suspicion and caution.

Notwithstanding all that, he put a huge amount of effort and hard work into playing the dealer and, more by luck than judgement, he did occasionally stumble across something of interest. Somehow he acquired the pattern books and other records of an old Sheffield cutler who had been famous in the nineteenth century for making Bowie knives. Included in the deal were several hundred blade blanks, also of the mid-nineteenth century.

Having studied the pattern book and the other records, he became very knowledgeable about both the company and its products. He also became aware that much of the cutlery industry involved outworkers who worked from their homes, some of whom he managed to trace. Richard prevailed upon them to hand grind and polish the blanks and to engrave them in the various styles as shown in the pattern books.

He also sought out people who made cross guards, scabbards etc. and put them to work. The outcome of all this effort was really well made, hand crafted Bowie knives with perfectly genuine Victorian blades, virtually impossible to tell from the originals. You might occasionally hear Bowie knife specialists say, 'I don't know if its a right one or one of Dickie Washer's specials.'

Would you believe the next thing our hero did, again with the aid of the pattern book and records, was to write a book about Victorian Bowie knives. Having done so, guess who the 'expert' is on the subject? People would consult Dickie about their Bowies and, bless him, he would, for a fee of course, authenticate them.

I still remember him with great affection whenever I hear someone say with great pride and certainty, 'Oh yes, it's a right one. It's illustrated in Richard Washer's book.'

Magazines

Leaving books but continuing with the printed word, let us consider the value of magazines. Most enthusiast and specialist magazines contain a lot of very useful information in articles by people who have many years of experience in one field or another and know what they are talking about. Unfortunately, it is not uncommon for the same magazines to carry articles by people who only *think* they know their subject and become authors when they finish their shift at the mill. The problem is sorting the wheat from the chaff, so be cautious.

Funnily enough, the older the magazines the better and more reliable the articles become. In pre-First World War copies of grand old magazines like *The Sphere*, it is quite usual to find, between 'Latest fashions' and 'Recipe of the Month', the most amazing articles on such diverse subjects as the Birmingham jewellery trade or the American clock industry, even write-ups on famous collections. So any pile of old magazines is worth checking.

I would suggest also looking for privately printed magazines of antiquarian or historical societies, but here, I do stress, the older they are the more reliable they will be.

Newspapers

Finally, alas, we come to newspapers. I think it was Sir Robert Marks, one-time commissioner of the Metropolitan Police, who said, 'Never believe anything you read in a newspaper except the date and check that with your diary.' My apologies to Sir Robert if I have got that wrong, but I wish I had said it.

It breaks my heart the number of times I have had old people come into my shop clutching some worthless bit of trivia because an idiot of a reporter has written an article saying it is much sought after and valuable. I only wish they and the editors who allow this sort of rubbish to be published were in my shop when I have to disillusion the poor old souls so that they could see the disappointment and unhappiness they cause.

What laughingly passes as a newspaper in the Portsmouth area has, at times, published an antique column written by an employee of one of the local auction houses. In my opinion, it is little more than an ongoing advertisement for the auction house concerned, with the advice to those with antiques to contact the writer at the business address of the auctioneers clearly printed at the end of each article. As the advice is being offered free and as a public service, I suppose that if as a result of the column the auction house were to be offered articles for inclusion in one of their sales, they would of course take the proper moral stand and refuse such articles. Remember the old business adage that there is no such thing as a free lunch. The same applies to so-called free advice.

As I understand it, it is now illegal to wrap fish and chips in newspaper. That being so, I cannot help but wonder what on earth is the point in publishing our local rag? One could, I suppose, light the fire with it – which is possibly about the best thing a collector could do with the type of advice contained in newspapers.

So where else might we look in our quest for knowledge?

Museums and Libraries

Much overlooked by many collectors are the research facilities and other services offered by museums. Remember it is not just a question of wandering around in the hope that some of the exhibits might touch on your particular subject. Many museums regularly lay on highly specialised exhibitions on such diverse subjects as Meccano sets, children's clothing and other themes which, on the face of it, you would not expect in that town or museum. So rather than just pay your entrance fee and wander around in the vague hope of spotting something on your subject, do take the trouble to ask for a list of forthcoming specialist exhibitions and events – one of them might be right up your street.

You would be well advised to consult your local museums department regarding the very wide range of services some of them provide for the guidance and enlightenment of the amateur collector and historian. These can include a whole range of lectures on specialist subjects, research facilities and, in the event of them not being in a position to help you, details of other museums that can.

Let me enlarge here on the subject of museums. They are in a way rather like icebergs in that only ten per cent is ever showing above the surface. To understand how this comes about, we need to look at a little bit of social history.

Up until the Second World War, many of the better-off individuals and families accumulated large collections of 'curios' on their travels, varying from the obscure to the obscene. As these people died off, the tendency was for their collections to be bequeathed to national and local museums where, as a rule, they were gratefully received. The museum displays in those days consisted mainly of strange and wonderful things from around the world, which the average member of the public, having never travelled, would normally never see in their lifetime.

The opportunities of world travel and the advent of TV, plus the arrival of 'political correctness' (whatever that is) have brought about huge changes in public tastes and fashion, and the museums have been greatly affected by this. The Elgin Marbles, Egyptian mummies and similar items are now the subject of much international wrangling and debate and Lord help any museum that exhibits 'Red Indian' or 'Eskimo' items instead of 'Native American' or 'Inuit'.

Because of all this, the policy now is for most local museums to concentrate on the history of their own area and all subjects relevant thereto. They still have, much to their embarrassment, the curios etc. that were inherited, but these are now consigned to the cellars. The best example of this is the large collection of erotica inherited by the British Museum, which can only be viewed by serious students of the subject by appointment.

What then we wonder does our local museum have hidden away? Could it be a collection of your field of interest and might it be available for viewing by serious collectors like you? You won't know unless you ask.

Remember these museum services are yours, as are many of the great national museums. It is your taxes that pay for their upkeep and the wages of their staff – they are there to serve you. What is more, in the main, they are eager and anxious to help and really want the public to use the services they provide.

One lady I know is constantly calling the Victoria and Albert Museum for advice on how to hang her tapestry or how to bring the colour back to a piece of furniture that has faded and other such questions. The V and A, bless them, seem to come up trumps every time. She thinks they are wonderful and they are happy to help her.

In your search for information, do use all these institutions. The Public Records Office, other archives and libraries are staffed by highly trained and professional people who know where and how to look for the information that you are after. One point to remember though: they are not trained to give valuations and quite rightly will not attempt to do so.

There are museums which are not in the same category of the above, such as those run by trusts on behalf of various military and business organisations. Most military museums are owned by trusts as are, for instance, the Cutlers of Sheffield or the London Livery Companies. Some smaller organisations are run by groups of like-minded people who get together to preserve some part of our heritage or another which is in danger of being lost: a building, a ship, even the odd aircraft. These organisations do not belong to you and any approach for information should be very much in the form of a polite request and it would help if it were accompanied by a small cheque towards their running costs.

There are a few privately owned museums which are run on a commercial basis and who, as with any other businesses, will happily provide you with any information you care to pay for.

Do not, I beg of you, do what some collectors do: when they acquire something made by a company still in existence, they phone that company and demand instant and detailed answers to a string of sometimes impudent questions. These people are running a business and have better things to do than to drop everything at the behest of some over-enthusiastic collector. A polite letter to the company secretary might have the required effect, again especially if accompanied by a small donation to the company's trade charity.

Clubs, Societies and Associations

The next source of information I am not at all sure about: clubs, societies and associations. On the one hand I suppose they do provide an opportunity for like-minded people with a shared interest to meet and exchange information via the club magazines and the monthly meetings. My experiences, however, also make me question the value of such information or indeed membership of such organisations. I think what bugs me most is not the individual members but the officers and committee members, with their much mistaken assumption that they are the final arbiters on all matters concerning the subject in which the organisation and its members are interested. Let me give you a few examples.

One very senior member of the legal profession, who was a member of a certain learned society, was discussing with me some of the more advanced collections in the area when, in passing, I mentioned a few important pieces that I knew of. He commented that he knew of no collection containing such items and I pointed out that the owner was a rather private person and probably did not belong to his society. At this he took great umbrage and told me in no uncertain terms that no serious collector could exist without the benefits of his society. When I told him that I knew of a number of very advanced collectors who did not belong to his society, he got quite heated and reminded me that he was of the legal profession and much used to dealing in facts and that I ought to do my homework before talking such rubbish. Not wishing to fall out with him – who knows, I might one day meet him in a professional capacity – I kept my peace. But, over the next few months, I had a word with my leading collectors as to whether or not they belonged to my learned friend's organisation and whether they thought he was right. The next time I met up with him, I asked him if he recalled our conversation. He did indeed and added something to the effect that he had never heard such nonsense. I told him what I had discovered. Of the dozen or so people with far more advanced collections than his own, nine had told me that they had never belonged to his society and had no intention of joining, two had belonged but had left as they felt it was of no benefit to them and one was still a member but did not attend the meetings.

One lovely young lady, on whom we had spent much time and effort in helping to start a modest collection, was handling a piece that we were none too happy about. 'I'll take this,' she announced. We explained to her that we would rather she didn't as we were not 100 per cent sure of the item. 'Oh, that's all right,' she announced blithely, 'I have joined a society and we have an approval committee who looks at anything we buy. Members of the committee decide whether it is right and if we have paid a fair price. If they say it is wrong, the dealer has to take it back or if we have paid too much the dealer has to adjust the price.' We asked her how the committee was made up and were there any professional dealers on it. 'No, it's just the more experienced members who meet once a month for this purpose.'

It took us an awfully long time to get through to her that no dealer worth their salt would be the slightest bit interested in the opinions of a committee of amateurs and would most certainly not permit themselves to be dictated to by such a committee.

Leaning against the wall of the shop behind the counter was a very nice muzzle-loading rifle, complete with its case and all accessories. In walked two of our heroes, association badges gleaming on their lapels. One, spotting the case, asked did it perhaps hold a Whitworth rifle. On being told that it did indeed, they immediately demanded to see it. It was explained to them, very politely, that the item was not in fact our property but only in for storage. Immediately, out came the membership cards and we were assured that, as members of the association, they were desperately keen to see the rifle even if it could not be bought. Much against our better judgement, we agreed they could look at it but please not to handle or mess about with it. The shop got a bit busy and it was only when things quietened down that we realised that they had left. Fearing the worst, we quickly checked that the gun was still on the counter and, to our great relief, it was. The gun and all the accessories were now scattered about the counter and smothered in finger marks. Every bit had to be thoroughly cleaned and returned to its correct place in the case, which took some considerable time. That done, the case and its contents were quickly locked up in the strong room where they should have been in the first place.

During the whole of their visit, these guys never once said please or thank you, indeed they did not even have the courtesy to say goodbye. Shocking bad manners you may say, but it did not end there.

Some days later, we received an envelope through the post. It contained a questionnaire regarding the full details of the gun. Who owned it? What was the number? How much was paid for it? And many more impertinent questions. Attached to the questionnaire was a piece of the association's notepaper, scribbled on which was, 'We are preparing a register of known Whitworths. Fill in and return immediately'. The only thing that was done immediately was the whole lot was consigned to the waste paper basket.

A little later in the week, I was called to the phone. 'My name is Smith; I am the secretary of the association. I sent you a questionnaire about a gun two of our members saw in your shop and you have not sent it back yet. We are in a hurry to complete our register and can't hang about. See to it at once, will you!'

Gentle reader, there is in this book some strong and highly colourful language. Believe me, it is nothing compared to what I said to that gentleman in the ensuing couple of minutes.

This sort of behaviour is fairly typical of the arrogance of not all but more than enough associations, some of their officers and too many of their members.

Professional Dealers

The very best sources of information and guidance are the long-established, professional dealers. By definition they are professionals and their very existence depends on their knowledge and professionalism. They would not still be in existence were it not for that deep and wide-ranging know-how. What they do not know they have the wherewithal to find out through either the extensive libraries that most maintain or the even more extensive circle of associates they have within the trade, each a specialist in his or her own field. It is not only a question of what they know, but also who they know who does. The most reliable thing about them is that, while they have the professionals' confidence in their own judgement, they do recognise their limitations. If they do not know the answer, they will tell you so and not give you the sort of flannel that some half-hard 'experts' would in the same circumstances.

Your problem, my friend, is getting them to share that hard-won knowledge, which has taken many years to acquire, with you. If, as I have advised in another part of the book, you have succeeded in building up a good relationship with one or more dealers, then part of that relationship will be the dealers' willingness to help you in any way they can, but there are rules to the game.

When you have just bought an item from a particular dealer, then it is right and proper that they should give you all the information they can on that particular item. If you are well-known to the dealer as a collector in a certain field through your regular dealings with him or her, then again you can rightly expect, as a regular customer, that extra bit of help and advice. They will, in all probability, do this without being asked, but it is a two-way flow brought about by mutual respect and trust. It is this very respect and trust that should make you think twice before overstepping the mark and putting all that very valuable goodwill that has taken years to build up in jeopardy by trying to take advantage of the dealer, using him or her as a source of information about goods which he or she did not supply. You will find more on how to get the best out of your dealers in another part of this book.

With the exception of the 'super fairs', I would strongly advise you against looking for knowledge among the 'boot sale bandits' and 'the blue rinse brigade', the sum total of whose knowledge could probably be written on the back of a postage stamp and still leave room for the Lord's Prayer and The Old Testament. The same can be said for most of the stall-holders at specialist fairs for postcards, militaria etc. The problem with these people is that what little they do know they get from fellow stallholders who are just as ignorant. The danger for the collector seeking information is that these 'weekend experts', being so insecure and unsure of themselves, will, rather than admit that they do not know something, make up the most ridiculous answers, which the poor innocent collector then takes as being correct. We in the trade call these silly stories 'fair fantasies'.

The most dangerous source of misinformation is the family friend who 'knows all about antiques'. The answer is simple: mostly, they don't. Remember, as I said earlier, if you meet someone who 'knows all about antiques', avoid them like the plague.

Television Shows

What about all the antique shows on TV? Yes indeed! *What* about all the antiques shows on TV. I could give you a very short, very rude answer, but since you have done me the courtesy of reading this book, I feel that some sort of 'health warning' is called for. What about 'Watching TV antiques shows can seriously damage your sanity'?

I believe that the original charter of the BBC charged the directors of that august body to 'amuse, entertain and educate the public'. I suppose, just as with the Teletubbies, these shows are entertaining, and both are pitched at about the same level of intelligence. Amusing they most certainly are. Educational they ain't! Let us take a long, hard, serious look at this particular phenomenon.

To understand the truth about these and other TV shows one has to know a bit about how they are made. Firstly, the producers have to keep them within a given budget, and then of course timing is all-important. The show must run for exactly a given number of minutes with, in the case of commercial television, the appropriate natural breaks to fit in the adverts, or it will run into the news or the next programme. Hence, a great deal of editing takes place, usually resulting in things being taken out of context and most of the full story ending up on the floor of the editing room. My own experience of this included hearing my voice over part of a programme in which I was not even involved and seeing a 15-minute interview that I had given reduced to about as many seconds. There is an old media adage, 'Never let the truth get in the way of a good programme'.

Remember always that TV people have one aim in life, that is good viewing figures. They will go to almost any lengths to increase their viewing figures for the very good reason that the higher the viewing figures the better the career prospects of the people involved in the making of that programme.

Let us look at the evidence in, for instance, the case of that well-loved institution, *The Antiques Roadshow*. We see long queues of hopefuls clutching their plastic bags, waiting patiently to get in. There are thousands of them but only a few get featured. Is this because only one item in thousands is worth showing? The producers might claim that there is not enough time to show all the wonderful discoveries, in which case why do they pad the show out with things from the local church or the various so-called experts talking about their private collections? What about values? I always wonder about people who tell you prices but never back their judgement with their own money. And the constant reference to auction? Has this, I ask, got anything to do with most of the 'experts' being employed by the various auction houses?

I wonder how many stolen items have appeared on the show and been claimed back by their rightful owners? The producers never tell us. One item I saw on a programme was possibly the property of the Crown and, as such, I wonder if it should have been in private hands? It was, in my opinion, very bad form to show it at all.

We are not told very much about the items the 'experts' have identified as rare and valuable which subsequently turn out to be nothing of the sort. Have the producers of *The Antiques Roadshow* ever published figures to show just how many of the items taken to these shows end up in the hands of the auction houses, which employ some of the 'experts' appearing in the show? How expert are the 'experts'? I know for a fact that one of my own fakes was passed as genuine at one of the shows. I cannot but wonder about others in different fields.

I have other points to make in other parts of the book but just think about this. On more than one occasion I have seen someone produce an item which the 'experts' have been unable to identify. They call the other 'experts' and, with much giggling, tell the owner that they have never seen one of these before. They then, in all seriousness, tell the owner that it is absolutely genuine and worth X thousand pounds. One cannot but wonder, since they have never seen such an article, how the devil can they know its value and that it is genuine.

As with many other TV programmes, it's all a lot of fun and provides untold pleasure to a lot of people, but these shows are of no value to the serious collector from the point of view of learning; indeed the opposite might be more the case.

Some of the so-called advice offered to collectors on TV programmes beggars belief. On one occasion, the 'expert' was advising the viewers to be 'assertive' and to leave the dealers in no doubt that they, the collector, knew exactly what they were looking at and what they were going to pay for it. I think it was on a *Meridian* TV programme that the tame 'expert' was telling the collectors what to look for and how to handle the dealers. The 'lady', and I use the term loosely, came over to me as being some sort of Irish tinker woman, more likely to be selling clothes pegs door to door than to be an antiques expert. Any collector daft enough to follow the advice offered and act in the aggressive, pushy way suggested would very rapidly have been shown the door of any decent antiques shop. Notice, if you will, that all these programmes are made at markets and fairs but never in proper shops with professional dealers.

'Yesterday I could not spell anteek, but today I are a expert'

27

I have seen two programmes which were good: one on the development of the gun and the other about art with Mr Keating. I suspect there might also be some good *Open University* programmes which could be worth looking into.

To sum up then, TV is not generally, in my opinion, a good source of information for the serious collector. As with all things, knowledge and experience are at the end of a long hard road, but I do hope that the advice I have given will help you along the way and also help you to avoid the potholes.

3

Funding the Collection

'I would love to collect but I can't afford to.' Rubbish! Anyone can afford to collect.

A frequent visitor to one of our establishments is a wonderful chap of late middle years who walks the city, summer or winter, in an old duffle coat many sizes too big for him and usually with the hood up. Hence, we have named him 'Rasputin'. He is, as our Islamic friends would say, 'touched of Allah' or, as we less kindly say, 'short of the full shilling!' Notwithstanding all this, Rasputin collects. Many a dull day is brightened by his arrival and inevitable question:

'' Ave yer got any?'

'No, sorry Rasputin, not today.'

'Orl right, bye bye.'

'Bye bye, Rasputin.'.

'Yer aven't got any'

'No Rasputin, bye bye.'

'Bye bye.'

After several more farewells, he departs.

Rasputin collects advertising pens. He has hundreds of them, all different, and if you offer him one that he already has, he will politely decline it, as indeed he will any that do not work. There are times when he is a bit of a nuisance, but I am not the only one who now pinches pens from hotel rooms and offices in the hope that it is a specimen that he does not already have! When I see the delight on Rasputin's face, I think I am as thrilled as he is. Not that it matters in the slightest, but I do sometimes wonder if the dear old fellow can actually write.

This gentleman's collection has cost him nothing in monetary terms, but a great deal of hard work and travel in his searches. I tell his story not in any derogatory way, indeed I hold him in higher esteem than many of the clever clogs with whom I deal, but simply to illustrate that one needs to be neither well-off nor a genius to collect.

The funding of any collection really should be a matter of common sense but, unfortunately, in practice, it very rarely is. We could perhaps paraphrase the Bible, 'Render unto Caesar the things that are Caesar's and unto God the things that are God's'. The rest after tax is yours.

That's not a bad way to look at it.

After you have paid the mortgage, fed the kids and sent a box of chocolates to old Aunt Matilda, whatever is left after meeting all your other obligations is fun money, to spend on fast women and slow horses or, if you are so minded, on building a modest antiques collection. You do not, however, under any circumstances, use the monies earmarked for the home and family for anything as unimportant as a collection. To do so is to court both financial and domestic disaster.

Please, dear reader, remember always that collecting is only a fun thing for your amusement in your spare time. Do not, I beg of you, let it become an obsession.

Many weaker people let their collecting become a psychological crutch for their failed egos. It has been said, sadly correctly, that collecting is in some cases a combination of greed and ego, the one constantly feeding on the other.

Ask yourself this. If you buy an item for £5 and it turns out to be worth £100, are you going to rush back and give the vendor the other £95? No, of course not. So, when the boot is on the other foot and you have paid over the odds, you can hardly start whinging about being ripped off and wanting your money back. That, my friend, is exactly why we only use spare cash on our collections.

One of the most widely-held misconceptions is that all antiques are a good investment. Absolute twaddle! Many items depreciate dramatically due to swings in fashion. Others are affected by economic pressures both in the UK and abroad. Yes, it is true that other things go up in value, sometimes equally dramatically, but the whole thing is a gamble. Nothing wrong with the odd gamble providing, of course, that we are not gambling with the kids' holiday money.

This whole misconception about investment is yet another example of the rubbish we see and hear on TV and in the newspapers. What the media people seem incapable of understanding is the question of inflation and buying power. Let me give you a couple of examples:

'Gosh!' the 'expert' exclaims, 'how did you come by that?'

The owner, 'the stare' all over his face, explains: 'Dad bought it in 1920 when we were in Cornwall on holiday. He paid £200 for it.'

'Today,' proclaims the 'expert', 'that is worth £40,000,' and adds, 'so that was a jolly good investment your father made!'

Who does he think he is kidding? Just think about it. At the height of the depression in 1920, anybody with £200 was well off. That sort of money then would have bought a semi-detached house or a row of coastguard cottages. Today, £40,000 wouldn't buy you one cottage. I doubt that it would even buy you a decent timeshare!

On another occasion, a client enquired whether or not I remembered some rather super Colt pistols that I had had in 1966. I assured him that I most certainly did remember them. At this stage, that awful smug look that some collectors adopt when they think that they know something that the dealer doesn't, came over his features and, with great glee, he produced a catalogue of a recent sale in which the same Colts had featured. 'Remember what you sold them for?' he asked. On being told about £250 each, the man informed me, with a malicious grin, 'Well, they made an average of £3,500 in the sale,' and added, 'bet you wished you had kept them as an investment.'

Both his grin and his delight at what he perceived to be my mistake rapidly diminished as I explained to him that, in 1966, £250 would have bought a new car or a third of a terraced house. Today, £3,500 would probably not buy a new car and only about a tenth of a terraced house, added to which was the considerable amount of money I had made by the use of that £250 over a period of 30-odd years. To have kept those pistols would have been anything but a good investment.

My experience leads me to believe that if you are looking for investment in purely financial terms, you would do far better to talk to your bank manager rather than an antiques dealer and, whatever you do, make sure you do not risk your pension fund in antiques.

The real and only lasting investment you will get from your collection will be the hours of pleasure you get from putting it together and the sheer enjoyment that having it will bring. I really do not think you can ask for a better return on your money than that.

'Ye ken, Mr Rothery. I have a drink problem.'
'Really Hamish?'
'Aye, I canae afford it!'

This illustrates a problem that many collectors and would-be collectors suffer from; basically their eyes are bigger than their bank accounts. They seem to get a fixation on some field of collecting that is completely beyond their financial ability, a fact that appears to be completely lost on them. They moan and groan to all and sundry about the scarcity of items which, even if they were available, they could not afford. This is also a fact they seem completely unable to grasp. The world does not owe anyone a collection and, to the best of my knowledge, they are not available on the National Health. Yet.

So, rather than moan about what we know we can't do, let's look at what we can do within our limited budget.

Having learnt a bit about our chosen field and armed with the few quid we have got, we could, over a period of time, find the odd near miracle bargain. Occasionally, it does happen. I know of a lady who has done exactly this with silver. She now has a small but rather nice collection, but it has taken her some 30 years to put together, a situation which she cheerfully accepts given her circumstances.

If this is a bit slow for you, why not consider the options I have outlined in Chapter 7. Another option, which many of my collectors have picked up on, is to seek out a subject which is not fashionable. Remember always that it is not the rarity or beauty alone which sets the prices on things, but how fashionable they are. Many items have, over the years, fallen out of fashion and a great many more have never been in fashion. Do please give it some thought and if something starts to interest you, go for it. Do not give a second thought for what anyone else thinks: 'What do you want to collect that rubbish for?', to which the answer is, 'Well, I'm not collecting it for you, so mind your own business.'

Two small points to remember if you do go down this path. If your chosen subject is not widely collected there are probably few, if any, books to refer to and you will be hard put to find anyone to give you any advice. There is, of course, always the chance that your subject might one day become fashionable, in which event your collection will become more valuable and you can write the only book on the subject which no one can argue with since they know even less than you do.

Cash and its definition can be the cause of a great deal of misunderstanding. Time and time again, collectors will look all conspiratorial and say, with a wink, 'How much for cash?' suggesting, I suppose, that the dealer is willing to conspire with them to cheat the VAT man or the Inland Revenue. No reputable concern will, of course, become involved with such criminal activity any more than they would deal in stolen goods or mug old ladies. All takings go through the books, be they cash or cheques. Such dubious activities do take place among the spivs and ne'er-do-wells at the bottom end of the market, but do please remember that anyone who cheerfully cheats the government and other bodies will equally cheerfully cheat you. One odd thing I have observed is that when some fly type bangs on about cash, when they've got a slight reduction they then invariably produce their cheque book.

Another manifestation of this enigma concerns my own regular customers. If, when they are buying something, I have the temerity to suggest that cash would be acceptable rather than a cheque, they become all hurt and upset that I apparently do not trust them enough to accept a cheque for a few hundred pounds. This, of course, is not the case. Rather, I have run out of cash and cannot get down to the bank to draw more should I need it to buy any items that might come in. Having been reassured that no offence was intended, they then pay by cheque and go on their way. On the odd occasion when I buy something from them, if I offer a cheque they look very sad, shuffle their feet and mutter, 'Well, I would rather have cash.'

Among collectors in general, there is an assumption that dealers will accept cheques from people who they do not know and who do not have a guarantee card for the required amount. They are quite put out when a dealer follows exactly the same procedures that the collector would apply in their own business. Double standards again or 'Ah, but that's different'?

When it comes to matters of money, the collector and the awful part-time dealer seem to live in cloud-cuckoo land. Time and time again, I have seen collectors go through a dealer's stock and then, completely unabashed, announce that they have no money. If they have no money on them to buy goods, why waste the dealer's time? Such peculiar behaviour is unlikely to endear them to the dealer in the future. Think about it. Who in their right mind ever leaves the house without some sort of buying capability, especially if you are a devout collector? You could at any time and in the most unexpected places find that item you have been seeking for years or the bargain of the century, neither of which you can buy because you have been daft enough to come out without any money. Surely, I hear you cry, the dealer will hold it for you. Oh no! Too many dealers have got into difficulties by holding goods for people who either come back weeks later or not at all. True, for a substantial deposit, a dealer might hold an article for an agreed time, after which, if not collected, the item will be returned to stock and the deposit, less a cancellation fee, credited. Not a lot of good though if you do not have the deposit on you. If you are an old customer with a good relationship with a dealer, he or she might hold something without a deposit, but you really are imposing on their goodwill. Please try to remember that dealers rely on turnover to make a living and they are not going to get much turnover if their capital is tied up for months in stock which has not been paid for. If your pet dealer is good enough to hold an item for you, it is a matter of common courtesy to complete the transaction as soon as possible. Should you for any reason have to delay collection, then a phone call explaining the delay would be much appreciated and would help to cement your relations with that dealer for future transactions.

Allow me to explain to you my personal approach to the subject of cash. Among the many peculiar habits I have developed over the years is the carrying of my 'buying float', the ready-use money that is always with me in case I stumble across a deal. Without the reassuring pressure of it in my hip pocket, I do not feel fully dressed, so much so that even in my own home when I change for dinner, knowing full well that I will not be leaving the house, I still put it in my pocket.

There was one famous occasion when we were celebrating

Burns Night (25 January). I, of course, was running late and the guests were due when my lady, entering my dressing room to hurry me up, found me carefully folding bank notes into my sporran. All that apart, it must be said that time and time again this habit of always having my float with me has paid dividends.

Once, having attended a dinner in London and then gone on to a nightclub, I found myself still in full evening dress at an early morning market in Islington. Despite being on the receiving end of a barrage of cockney humour, I made a number of very profitable purchases, a feat which would not have been possible had I not had the foresight to put my buying float in the tail pocket of my coat before setting out for the evening.

To give you some less exotic examples, on my way to lunch one Sunday, I stopped to buy flowers for my hostess and spotted a very desirable piece in the antiques shop next to the florist. Having my float on me and the shop being open, I was able to purchase it on the spot. Another time when returning late at night from dinner with a friend, I stopped at a garage to fill up with petrol. The attendant, seeing a sword, which I had taken for my friend's opinion on the back seat of the car, asked if I was interested in that sort of thing as he had some similar items that he wished to dispose of in his house next to the garage. He did, of course, want cash. The outcome was that I bought a nice bundle of bits and a few weeks later the guy phoned me with another lot he had found. When I bought the second lot I asked if nobody locally had wanted to buy his goods, to which he replied, 'Yes, but you don't mess about and you pay immediately in cash.' On a lesser scale, I doubt that a week goes by when I am shopping in the village and do not buy something or other thanks to my having the buying float with me.

Returning with Dave Crabtree from an auction somewhere near Egham, we were passing through a village when Crabbers suddenly gasped, 'Stop, I feel sick.' I quickly pulled in by a terrace of shops and he dashed up an alleyway and proceeded to be violently ill in a convenient dustbin. I followed to see if he was all right and he said he was but asked to be left alone for a minute or two. I stationed myself at the end of the alley where I would not intrude on his misery but could watch him in case he passed out. As I stood there, I realised that I was standing outside a small china shop and could see the butt of a musket just showing behind a cabinet. Checking that Dave was still OK, I nipped in and the lady told me it was not her sort of thing but, while she hated having it in the shop, she had reluctantly agreed to try to sell it for a friend who wanted £20 for it. Knowing I could get £40 for it, I hastily paid her the money and put the gun on the back seat of the car, then looked again to see how Dave was getting on. He was staggering back up the alley towards the car, white-faced and sweating. On reaching it, he leaned heavily against it while he recovered. Suddenly, he spotted the musket on the back seat and stood upright, the colour rapidly returning to his face. 'You bastard, Rothery. You took advantage of my being ill to go and have yourself a deal. What sort of a mate are you to do a thing like that?' Completely ignoring his malaise, he kept on in this vein all the way back to Portsmouth. Of course we shared the profit, but it was a story we both enjoyed telling for years after.

This then is another example of where my ready-use buying float came to the fore. Even if that china lady had been willing to hold the musket for me, it would have involved me in making a long return journey to collect the gun and pay for it.

There are those reading this who are thinking, 'What a fool to carry cash on him all the time, he might get mugged'. Possibly, but never in 50 years have I felt the slightest bit at risk and, among the many dealers I have asked, none have ever heard of it happening. Obviously one would never flash the money about in a bar or at a boot sale where footpads and the like might lurk. It must be said that there have been occasions when some silly arse has lost or mislaid their money and one genius of a part-time dealer actually managed to sell a jacket off his stall with both the float and the day's takings in the pocket!

The biggest problem that I and other dealers have is finding enough stock to satisfy the demands of our clients. We cannot afford to miss any opportunity to buy in any worthwhile items that are available. Very simply, if we do not buy we have nothing to sell, and if we have nothing to sell we go under. The slight risk of carrying modest amounts of money is preferable to missing any opportunity to buy stock. To put it as simple arithmetic, had I lost or had stolen £5,000 over the years, it would be nothing in comparison to the profits I have made by always having the ability to take advantage of any deal that came along.

As always, the TFIs of the world are the worst offenders as they, with monotonous regularity, wander into shops, select items and announce that as usual they have no money on them and will collect tomorrow or Monday. In their abysmal ignorance it would not occur to them to ask if the shopkeeper minded. They rarely do come back tomorrow or Monday but days if not weeks later they return and, in their airy-fairy manner announce that they have come to pick up the item that has been put aside for them. If challenged as to why they did not come in when they said they would, they then say they forgot or were busy. I suspect the truth is that they have been waiting for their giro from the DSS. It probably does not cross their tiny minds that the dealer has had to carry that item for weeks without payment.

Eventually of course, the dealers get to know who these idiots are and any worthwhile pieces smartly disappear on their approach. Personally, on the very rare occasions that I put anything aside for a client, I make it quite clear that Monday *means* Monday. If the item is not collected by end of business, it goes back into stock and I do my damnedest to make sure it is sold before Chummy comes in again, on which occasion I advise them never again to ask for an item to be put away for them.

What has all this got to do with you, the collector? You are not, of course, under the same pressures as the dealer to buy. But it must be most frustrating and annoying to any collector who, having found the thing for which they have been looking for years, is unable to buy it because the dealer does not have the facilities to take credit cards or your guarantee card is only for £50 and he or she will not hold the item without a deposit. Please do not blame the dealer. He or she is running a business and applying normal business practice. If your guarantee card has too small a limit and you do not have the cash to purchase the item or put down a proper deposit, you have no one to blame but yourself.

Many people will write a cheque for several hundred pounds and then offer a guarantee card with a £50 limit. When the dealer refuses to accept this they throw a tantrum. When I get these situations in the shop and ask the clients why on earth they go into shops without money, I get the wet answer, 'Well, I didn't expect to buy anything.' I am not sure whether this is a reflection on my stock or their state of mind.

If you want to avoid all this silliness, why not always carry sufficient cash to enable you to put down a sensible deposit – 10 per cent is usually the norm – should you come across the thing for which you have been looking for ages. It's a better idea than losing the thing that you have taken years to find.

Contrary to general belief, most dealers are very reasonable and accommodating people, and as well as holding goods against a deposit, some will even let customers pay for an item via several payments over a more extended period, and collect the goods when the last payment is made. Do bear in mind that star customers get star treatment, including special privileges not normally extended to the general public. One final point on the question of goods being held for you: you would be ill-advised to haggle over the price and then expect the dealer to wait for his money.

Whilst on matters of finance, I suppose we should look at the vexatious subject of haggling. This thoroughly unpleasant and degrading practice was much indulged in between gypsy horse traders and secondhand car dealers in the old days and is now regrettably becoming the norm amongst collectors and the bottom end of the fringe dealers. The most avid hagglers are invariably people in nice safe jobs such as the civil service or local government, where they enjoy a secure income with annual increments and can look forward to an index-linked pension at the end of their working lives. Not satisfied with all of this, these greedy people take great pleasure in trying to screw those who are not so swathed in cotton wool out of a decent return on their investment and hard work.

The most common example in my own shop is when newly-commissioned naval officers come in looking for swords. Most of them then proceed to haggle like backstreet traders and I cannot help but feel that among the many subjects taught at Britannia, they should perhaps include good manners. Most people, when challenged as to why they always want to haggle when they would never dream of haggling in their own job, come out with one of two silly answers: 'Well, you've got to ask,' or 'Well, that's the fun of it.' No, you do *not* have to ask and, if you think haggling is fun you probably need some sort of professional counselling.

Let us look at a couple of examples of this odd syndrome in practice. During one of the many TV programmes on antiques, the presenter simpered, 'Don't forget to haggle', so, notwithstanding the fact that I had seen the lady on other programmes, during which she appears to drink rather a lot, I took her advice.

'BBC.'

'Can I speak to the director general, please?'

Stunned silence.

'Hold the line, please.'

'BBC duty officer here, who is calling?'

'My name is Rothery. May I speak to the director general, please?'

'I am afraid that's not possible, can I help you?'

'I am following the advice of your presenter who is telling the public to always haggle. Who do I speak to about a deal on my TV licence?'

'Ah, but that's different.'

It usually is when you try to haggle with the hagglers!

Two middle-aged well-dressed gentlemen sat quietly drinking in the bar of a restaurant, discussing the décor which was of a naval theme of the Napoleonic era. The head waiter approached them and enquired if they were thinking of dining. The two gents' eyes met and, with that affinity which only exists between old friends, an unspoken message passed between them.

'Well, we might. Do please bring us the menu to look at.'

'Certainly, sir.'

'Perhaps you would bring us the wine list as well,' said the other gent.

'With pleasure, sir.'

After a while, the waiter returned to enquire if the gentlemen had made a decision. A lengthy discussion regarding the make-up of the various dishes and the merits of the wine ensued. Finally, it was decided. A dozen oysters from Arcachon with a bottle of Chablis, followed by beef Wellington with a red Rioja. If there was room for a pudding, maybe a soufflé with a glass of Chateau Yquem.

The waiter scribbled all this down and was about to depart for the kitchen when one of the gents asked, 'How much does all that come to?'

Somewhat taken aback, the waiter did a quick calculation. 'Two hundred and forty pounds, sir.'

'How much can you do that lot for?' asked the gent.

'What do you mean, sir?' asked the now rather confused waiter.

'Well, what's your best price?'

'The prices are on the menu, sir.'

'Yes, but how much will you give us off for cash?'

The professional smoothness of the young waiter was rapidly disintegrating, when a knowing look spread across his face and he looked around in a conspiratorial manner.

'You gentlemen are from one of those TV shows. Come on, where are the hidden cameras?'

'No, young man, we are deadly serious. Perhaps you should fetch the proprietor.'

The waiter grinned, 'Oh, you're friends of Mr Jones.'

Off he scuttled to return a few minutes later with a red-faced and none-too-pleased Mr Jones.

'What the devil is going on?' he demanded.

'Do you not recognise us?' asked one gent.

'No, why should I?' snarled the by now apoplectic proprietor.

'Well, we are two of the dealers from whom you purchased most of the décor of this establishment.'

'So what?' exploded Mr Jones.

'So now we are doing to you what you have been doing to us for the last six months!'

So endemic has this awful practice become that even reputable dealers now sometimes put a little extra on the price just to knock it off again as a sop to the ego of the hagglers. All in all, it is as I said earlier, a most vexatious problem and I am not at all sure of how I may best advise you. Mostly the answer lies in good old common sense. At boot sales and fairs, the stallholders will in all probability be only too happy to haggle, it being in their nature to do so. They are not, however, a reliable source of supply. For reliability and safety we rely on our regular, established dealer and we do not want to prejudice our much-treasured relationship with them by behaving in their shop in the same way we might at boot sales and fairs.

Think along these lines. Firstly, no dealer *has* to haggle, either legally or by choice, and indeed many, myself included, do not generally do so. Not that we are mean, but it is hard enough to get good stock in the first place without mugging it away when we do get it. Remember, with antiques, especially the rarer pieces, it is not like buying an electric toaster where you know the list price, can try several shops to get the best deal, and if Curry's haven't got one you can try Comet who might even order you one. If you are looking for a very rare Nagasaki bus stop and you have the good fortune to find one, you can't in all probability find another in the same country, let alone up the road, and you most certainly can't order one up like a toaster. So if you want the one you have found, you would be foolish to risk losing it by trying to haggle with the dealer. The dealer, of course, is fully aware of this situation. He has a highly desirable piece and possibly several people after it, one of whom he knows will buy it sooner or later. Why on earth should he take less than the price he is asking?

I think here we have another of those misconceptions that some collectors suffer under: that all dealers are desperate to make a sale. True, they need to make sales to survive, but not to the extent where they are not going to make a decent profit. There are a couple of trade sayings on the subject: 'turnover is vanity and profit is sanity' and 'when a deal is no longer profitable, turn your back on it and walk away'. These days, most established dealers can afford to do just that.

When buying from your regular dealer, they will probably 'look after' you on the prices without being asked. I feel sure that when this happens and you are given a special price you would not be stupid and greedy enough to ask for more. If, on the other hand, you are in a strange shop then ask the person you are dealing with whether the price is negotiable. If they politely tell you no, then it is up to you whether you buy it or not. Whatever you do, for goodness sake, do not do what I consider to be one of the stupidest things that I have ever seen collectors do, and that is to not buy an item solely because the dealer refuses to haggle. Dozens of times I have seen people leave perfectly good and sometimes exceptionally good items at reasonable and even cheap prices because they take umbrage at the dealer's refusal to lower an already reasonable price. Again, it is the ego getting the better of common sense.

Finally, do remember this, that if the dealer wants £100 for an item, that is what you are going to pay, whether you and the dealer play this silly game of haggling or not. Here is an example:

Nice shop with good stock nicely displayed and clearly priced. Shopkeeper, bright-eyed and bushy-tailed, behind the counter, ready for the day's business. In walks Joe Public.

'Good morning, sir.'

No reply.

Five minutes pass.

Shopkeeper tries again. 'Good morning, sir. Can I help you?'

'No.' A pause. 'Just looking.'

After a further five minutes, Joe speaks. 'What have you got on that old picture up there?'

Shopkeeper runs his finger along the frame. 'Rather a lot of dust I'm afraid, sir.'

'Can I see it?'

'I hope so, sir, but would you like me to move the light along a bit?'

'No, I want to see it.'

'Oh, you want to handle it!'

The picture is removed from the wall and placed on the counter. Joe tries to look intelligent.

'It's slightly faded.'

'Yes, sir, it's very old.'

'There is a small crack in the frame.'

'Yes, sir, the frame is also very old.'

'What are you asking for it?'

'I would prefer pounds sterling, sir.'

'No, how much is it?'

'The price is written on the label, sir.'

'It says £150.'

'Well done, sir.'

'What's your best?'

The shopkeeper is somewhat confused. 'Well, sir, it's a rather nice three-piece pinstripe that I had made in Sackville Street and with it I usually wear a...'

'No, can you do a better price?'

'That's most kind of you, sir, but I would be perfectly satisfied with the £150. I really do not want more.'

'Bert Smith sells this sort of picture for £70.'

'Then perhaps you should buy off him.'

'He hasn't got any.'

'When I haven't got any, mine are £50 but when I've got them, they are £150.'

'Will you take £100?'

'No, sir.'

'Why not?'

'Because, if I had wanted £100, I would have priced it at £100.'

Joe leaves the shop and the picture is returned to the wall.

Both Joe Public and the shopkeeper are completely bemused by the antics of the other. So, what's it worth? 'An antique is worth what it's worth to the person who wants it'. You will hear this said time and time again and, in the main, it is true. But at the same time, we none of us want to pay over the odds for an item no matter how much we desire it. Let me give you a few ideas as to how you could work out the sort of price you would be comfortable with. Remember always, price is what you pays, quality is what you gets!

The first thing is to forget about getting bargains all the

'What do you think that is then?'
'Fifty quid.'

time. You will get them occasionally but you will also pay too much occasionally. Over the years, the two will probably even out and you will find that on average you have paid about the going rate overall.

If you are a proper collector and not just a bargain hunter, the majority of your collection will cost about the going rate existing at the time you buy it, so what is the going rate? The only answer to that you will find by visiting as many dealers as possible, comparing them and working out an average. If you then see an example well below the average price but a bit tired, or an absolute cracker at well above the normal price, the decision is yours: it's worth what it's worth to the person who wants it – in this case, you. The point is that you know you are paying over the odds, but it is your choice to do so, not someone else's. The reverse is that you are not buying an inferior specimen because a guide says that it is cheap, but because you have made the conscious decision that, cheap or not, you do not want it in your collection.

The sort of thing that often crops up in the shop is, when I offer a person £100 for an item they tell me that some robbing so-and-so only offered them £50. They are surprised when I tell them that the other guy is not a robber but probably thinks he has offered a fair price and would, in all likelihood, sell it on for £65. The same thing happens in reverse when I offer them £100 and they tell me that they have been offered £150. It is not a case of me robbing them and I am not 'being funny' when I tell them to take the other guy's offer. It is no more than a matter of opinion. If you are told by a dealer or a friend that the price of an item should be X but they neither want to buy it nor have one to sell, then that

'No. I am getting 22 other prices and if you have been daft enough to offer more than anyone else, I'll let you have it.'

valuation is worthless since they cannot back it with the goods or they are not prepared to back their opinion with their money.

It is often said that 'beauty is in the eye of the beholder'. This could equally be applied to value being in the eye of the buyer. A fellow dealer, for whom I had the greatest respect, once bought a bundle of goods from me for £500. Included in the bundle was a pair of pretty little muff pistols by Cogswell and Harrison which I had put in at £120. Some weeks later, a client asked me to do an official valuation and produced the very same pistols, at the same time telling me that he had paid £90 for them. Obviously this could not be right. I knew my friend would never sell them at that since he had paid me much more, so I made an excuse to hang onto the pistols for a few days and took his name and address. On contacting my friend to ask if perhaps the pistols had been stolen, I was completely taken aback when he informed me that everything was in order and he had sold them to that gentleman for that price. He then explained to me that, whilst he had accepted the bundle at £500, he had only seen the pistols at £70 but the other items in the bundle at more, hence he had sold them for £90.

We had both agreed that the bundle as a whole was worth £500 but completely differed on the value of the individual items. No one was hurt and indeed, everybody was perfectly happy, especially the guy who had bought the pistols when I offered him a £10 profit which he took. I then sold them on for £125 to a collector who was over the moon with both the pistols and the price he had paid. Further joy and happiness all round and it goes to prove that value is very much in the eye of the buyer.

As we entered an establishment at a prearranged time, we were confronted by the proprietor being harangued by a rather loud and aggressive person.

'I'll give you £120.'

The shopkeeper declined the offer.

'Here, look!' the loud one counted the money onto the table. The proprietor again declined and pushed the proffered money back.

'You must excuse me,' nodding towards us, 'but this lady and gentleman have an appointment.'

The yob picked up his money and made to leave. On reaching the door, he bellowed, 'Do you want my money or not?'

'No, thank you.' the shopkeeper repeated icily.

I left the buying to my assistant and when she had completed her purchases and was about to settle up, the proprietor offered her the item that had been under discussion earlier.

'I think that at £120 I wouldn't get a profit on that,' she said.

'I agree,' said the proprietor, 'would £80 be acceptable?'

Having paid and loaded up we moved on. As we did so my assistant expressed surprise at the shop owner's actions and was even more surprised when I explained to her that in all probability the loud one wouldn't have got the item had he offered even more than £120.

Donkey's years later, that same young lady took great pleasure in relating to me how, when she was having a sale at our Scottish branch, she had refused a derisory offer from a particularly obnoxious and greedy person and then, to his delight and amazement, sold the same item to a nice young man for a lot less. It seems to me that there is a small proportion among collectors whose arrogance is such that they believe their unpleasant attitude and bad manners become acceptable, providing they spend a little money. Believe me, dear reader, they are very much mistaken.

This might seem to be an odd subject to bring up in the value section of a book about antiques collecting, but have you ever given any thought to the value of the time you spend in the pursuance of your hobby? From the purely monetary point of view, could you, as many collectors do, generate more funds to spend on your collection by doing a bit of overtime or extra work in your normal job? Or do you get more fun from taking a day off work and travelling some distance at considerable expense to track down an item, even though it has cost you, with expenses and a day off work, £120 on top of the cost of the item to do so? I mention this because I often get cases where the collector is moaning that the cost of collecting is high and they cannot afford some of the things they would like, but cheerfully use up valuable funds on travel or taking time off work. The other point of view is as with the man at the boot sale, who would pay £25 to get out of the house and does not even consider the time taken as anything but pleasure time.

There is a question of what an item is worth in different fields of collecting. For example, a death plaque from the First World War, which would normally sell at a few pounds in the medal world, actually made £850 at a literary memorabilia sale because it was named to Rupert Brooke, the poet. Similarly, the silver court sword I mentioned earlier was worth to the silver collector four times what it was worth to a sword collector.

If you are looking for a book about collecting, the bookshops may sell it cheap because the dustcover is missing or a bit rough, but to a student the contents are more important than the condition. You could, if you felt so disposed, make a study of the market and use it to your best advantage. I used to do this quite a lot with the silver trade. They wanted tea services but were not the slightest bit interested in silver with military inscriptions which, in my part of the trade, I could sell very well. I found the same with some of the china people. They were not interested in old plates with the crests of long forgotten regiments, but my military people were.

While researching my family history, I found that a distant relative of mine from Leeds married a very famous silhouettist by the name of Miers, way back in the 1790s. I do not, as a rule, like silhouettes but thought, in the circumstances, I should have a specimen of his work as part of the family history. Eventually I heard that one of his works was coming up in a local auction, together with a couple of lesser pictures as one lot. I asked my contact what the reserve was and he told me £60–£70. Well, it was worth a lot more than that to me, so I told him to buy it.

'What, even if it reaches two or three hundred?'

'Yes, buy it.'

When we met a few days later he informed me that it had gone to £340 so he had let another other guy have it. I was most put out as I thought I had told him to buy it at almost any price. He, on the other hand, thought that the sum mentioned of two or three hundred was my limit. I explained to him why I had wanted the picture and asked him that if he saw the purchaser, would he ask him if he would take a profit, as to me it was worth a lot more money. Sure enough, he phoned me a few days later and told me that he was with the purchaser who was willing to sell me the Miers for £700. I had thought that this chap would have been satisfied with £100 or so quick profit plus the other two items, but wanting to double his money was, in my opinion, being downright greedy, so I declined his offer.

On making enquiries, it turned out that even at £700 the picture was reasonable and should another come up I might have to pay more! Well, I still want a Miers so I suppose I'll have to pay whatever it takes to get one.

Let us use this example of my crass stupidity to examine what that silhouette or any other antique is worth.

To the auctioneer it, together with the other two bits, was worth £60–£70. On the day, because of my family connection, to me it was worth £500–£600. My man at the sale did not think it was worth more that £340, so I lost it and the other guy got it. Having got it, the new owner wanted £700. I, not thinking about what it was worth but indulging in a tantrum because I thought the guy was being greedy, refused it. He, in all probability, sold it for more and I am left still wanting a silhouette by Miers for which I am now willing to pay up to £1,000. If anyone had asked any of the participants in the above saga what a silhouette by Miers was worth, they would have got from very knowledgeable people a wide variety of honest but highly conflicting answers. Perhaps that old saying should be modified to 'an antique is worth what it's worth to the person who wants it, at the *time* they want it'.

The story of the silhouette also illustrates the danger that arises of missed opportunities where, because we are too concerned about the price, we forget to weigh up whether or not we are likely to ever get another chance to acquire the object of our desire at any price. You have heard it said often, 'This guy had a super Nagasaki bus stop, it was a bit pricey but I have always regretted not buying it,' to which is sometimes added, 'and I have never seen another one that I liked as much.' I most certainly have said it.

He who hesitates is lost! And what makes most collectors hesitate is, 'Might I find another in better condition or for less money?' Yes, you might. So, if you find a better specimen, it isn't a problem. You just buy it and get rid of the first one.

The answer to the second part of the saying was in a conversation I once overheard:

'Here, Fred. You know that thing you bought last year for £500? Well, the shop up the road has got one for £450. You should have hung on, mate.'

'Not really, Bert. I've had an extra year's pleasure from it and that's worth more than £50 to me.'

We could, or even should, add to the original saying, '…or we might never see another'. If you see the object you want but it is more than you wanted to pay, do not hesitate: buy it. You can always find another fifty quid but you may never find another such object for years, if at all, and you will always regret losing the item far more than spending the extra fifty quid. Remember always, you are the man who wants it, so its worth what its worth to you.

One of the old-timers gave me an excellent piece of advice when he told me, 'Always remember, Rothery, you are buying the item, not the story.' I am ashamed to admit that I have, on too many occasions, forgotten his advice and let the story affect my judgement as to the value of an object, invariably to my cost. The usual story is what the item cost the vendor. The guy with a blow-wave and a flash suit at the posh antiques fair: 'Dear lady, I had to pay £5,000 for it so I am only asking a modest £1,000 profit.' The knocker boy: 'On my baby's life, guvnor, I gave 'undred for it.' Both are, in all probability, lying through their teeth. These stories are no more than ploys used by the more dubious dealers to make the collector think that they are getting a good deal. No dealer of any standing would even think of discussing what they paid for an item with anyone other than the person from whom they bought it. If you think the object to hand is worth £500 to you, then whether the vendor paid £5 or £5,000 is completely irrelevant. You might, as I have, quite wrongly feel resentment at the profit the guy is making, or smug at the thought that you are getting something for less than someone else paid. Both attitudes have absolutely nothing to do with the value of the thing.

There are some collectors who have the impudence to ask dealers what they paid for an item, or make the stupid comment, 'I bet you didn't pay as much as that.' The dealers can be forgiven if the nice ones reply, 'I think that is between me and the person I bought it from, sir.' Or the less polite ones, 'Mind your own bloody business, sir.' Dave Crabtree's reply, which I must admit I often use myself, was usually, 'I paid £1 for it,' to which he would sometimes add, 'but I am selling it for £5,000.' The fact remains that if you think the item is worth X, then that is what it is worth to you, regardless of the stories of who paid what last week.

Again, I must ruefully admit to you that on more occasions than I care to remember I have let my judgement be coloured by both my ego and by completely irrelevant stories. It was once said that one of the advantages of getting old is you can give to other people the good and sound advice which you yourself have ignored.

The other type of story is what some posers like to call provenance. Again, mostly a lot of bull-shine or hearsay, as the legal profession like to call it. At the lower end of the market, it in no way affects the price of an item. If it's worth £50, it's marked £50, regardless of the stories that have passed through the vendor's family for generations.

Should the item be of great historic importance, that, of course, is an entirely different matter but the provenance needs to be researched just as deeply as the item itself. If the object and its provenance are proved to be genuine, then you most certainly will be buying both the object and the story.

I could write another book on the different attitudes to the question of 'what's it worth?' but here are some examples of what I have found over the years.

It is quite common for older people in the shop to comment on the prices of today in comparison to what they remember. Such was the case with a good friend of mine who listened patiently to an old boy talking about prices before the war and his comments that he used to buy the various pistols for two or three shillings. My friend commented that if sir still had them he would pay a lot more today.

'Matter of fact, I still have one.'

'Well, bring it in.'

Good as his word, a few days later the gentleman brought it in and on inspection it was found to be one of a pair of rather nice duelling pistols. My friend did not wish to lose it but also did not wish to pay too much and had no idea what the old boy was expecting. Finally, he said 'Twenty-five.'

The vendor replied, 'Rather! I only paid half a crown in '39!'

My friend counted out 25 crisp £1 notes and laid them alongside the pistol.

The old boy looked at them and said, 'What's that then?'

Thinking the chap was going to change his mind, my pal grabbed the pistol and shoved it under the counter, commenting, 'Twenty-five pounds, as we agreed.'

The old boy grabbed the money and put it quickly in his pocket. 'Blimey, I thought you meant 25 shillings!'

Returning from a trip down west, I called on a dealer I didn't like much; a bit flash. He produced a pair of pistols which he had bought at auction together with a rather nice small sword and boasted he had got the lot for £90. He said he would take a quick profit and I could have the pistols for £110 and he would keep the sword, worth about £75. The thought of him making £80 or £90 profit overnight when I was flogging my guts out to earn £30 a week annoyed me so I refused them and left. Twenty odd miles down the road, common sense reasserted itself and I realised that, regardless of what he was making, there was still £40 or £50 profit to be made on the pair. Turning the car, I went back and, completely ignoring his snide remarks about me not being able to recognise a good deal when I was offered one, paid him his £110.

For some weeks, the pistols remained in my shop priced at £145 and, although a lot of people looked at them, no one wanted to buy them. Eventually, I asked Ronnie Dufty, who had been staying with me, to take them back to Birmingham and put them in the next auction. To everybody's amazement, including my own, they made £1,250. Remember if you will that auction houses were not so greedy in those days, so I got back after charges about £1,100. This, at a time when terraced houses were changing hands for about £900 and I was taking £30 a week out of the company as wages.

The next time I called at the vendor's shop, his wife, who was a lovely lady, told me with some embarrassment that the guy had heard of my good fortune and felt that I should share the profit with him, say half and half. I left a message for him that as he had not shown this same sharing spirit when I bought the pistols, I felt disinclined to agree with him. The next visit to his establishment was my last as I was informed on my arrival that I was no longer welcome there.

Please do bear in mind that the prices mentioned in the various stories are those that existed at the time that the events took place.

A young friend of mine was studying at one of the London teaching hospitals and, as with most students in those days, he was constantly short of money. Indeed, his landlord had recently increased the rent of his small flat in Portchester Mews from £2 10s a week to £3. He resolved his financial problems by persuading a lady stallholder on the Portobello Road to allow him to use a corner of her stall. Each Saturday he would place a small cloth-covered tray full of inexpensive antique-style earrings and brooches there, priced at between 5s and 7s 6d per item. His takings never exceeded £10 even on a good week so, being a bit confused, I asked him how on earth he made any money. His answer was amazingly simple.

He would go to Woolworths in Oxford Street and buy these bits of jewellery for about 1s 9d and 1s 11d, take them to Portobello, put them on the tray at 5s or 7s 6d and sell most of his stock in a few hours. This earned him an average £5 net profit per week, which paid his rent and left him with £2 for a week's food and a few drinks.

My own experience of Portobello Road resulted in my having to stay well away from it for some months, through no fault of my own but for fear of retribution being wreaked upon me. I had purchased some 20 bugles at 5s each at a military surplus sale. When I got them back to the shop, it was found that they were all dated between 1918–1919, in those days far too modern for anyone to be interested in them, even at the modest 10s each for which I was offering them. In conversation with a friend in Hackney, I mentioned my problem and he suggested that the obvious thing to do would be to remove the dates. Further than that, as he was a shooter, why not remove the dates by putting a musket ball through them?

Eventually, I collected the modified bugles, now each sporting a jagged hole where the dates once were and, after much joking about each one being in the Charge of the Light Brigade, put them in the boot of the car and headed off to see Jimmy Goode at Portobello.

On arrival, it struck me that I should show Jimmy one of my bugles, so I got one out of the boot and set off with it clutched firmly in my hand. I had no sooner turned the corner than a gentleman accosted me, asking to see the item I was carrying. Saying not a word, I held it up for his inspection and he immediately offered me £5 for it, which I accepted. The transaction completed, he departed down the Portobello Road with his purchase and I with my £5 back to the car to get another bugle to show Jimmy.

For the next hour, every time I went to see Jimmy I was stopped by people who offered me from £3–£6 for the bugle I was carrying until my entire stock was exhausted. I didn't bother to see Jimmy but departed the scene clutching the best part of £100, most of which was profit. As I said earlier, I didn't go back to Portobello for the next few months.

How's this for an example of free enterprise? I was talking to a lady who told me that, having been widowed and seeking both an additional source of income plus an interest at weekends, she had become a stallholder at boot sales and the smaller fairs. I commented that it was not my idea of a fun weekend and an awful lot of work for very little return.

'Oh no,' she informed me, 'not the way I did it.'

She then explained that she would book a table at these events then, armed with the couple of hundred quid she had scraped together, she would arrive early and buy from the other stallholders as they were setting up until she had enough stock. Then she would mark up her purchases and commence business. By the end of the day, she had usually made £100 or so on the goods she had bought in the morning. She would then sell any surplus to the guy on the next stall for a few pounds and depart with her profit, having not had the problem of bringing or taking stock to and fro, or the hassle of looking for stock during the week.

I congratulated her and expressed the hope that long may she continue.

'No,' she said, 'I don't do it any more. Some of the other stallholders complained and I've been banned.'

Well, that certainly sounds like the small-mindedness typical of most of the stallholders I've met.

4

The Hunting Grounds

Armed with our new found knowledge, bubbling over with enthusiasm and with our budget fixed firmly in our minds, where do we start to look for the treasures that are going to form our collection?

In this chapter, I shall try to look at the various hunting grounds and evaluate their advantages and disadvantages, at the same time warning you of the dangers that lie in wait for the unwary. To do this, I need to explain the workings and background of 'the trade'. It is only when you know how the system works that you can use it to your advantage, so do please bear with me.

In the days before greed became so much a part of daily life, if it was known in the family that somebody was a collector, uncles and aunts would dig out interesting items and give them to that budding collector. Today, they are more likely to sell such items to them, but only after making sure that they are getting the market price. It is only when they are certain that an item has no market value that they are likely to donate it to their niece or nephew's collection.

It is very common for a dear old lady to bring in a box of odds and ends and explain that somebody in the family wants them but they want to know if they are worth anything first and to be assured that they are not giving away a fortune. Having been so assured, they toddle off quite happily. It is fair odds that within the next couple of days the same box of bits in the hands of a young hopeful will reappear in the shop with, ''Ere mate, my auntie give me these. They worth anything?'

In the same vein, but slightly different, we have an amusing situation with a box of items which, over the last 20 years, has become a regular visitor. Each time an elderly person will bring the box in and enquire as to its value, at the same time explaining that an old friend has left it to them. We can only assume that, having been assured that it is not of any great value, they in turn leave it to another old friend, rather like a ghostly game of 'pass the parcel'.

Having said all that, it might be worth letting relatives or friends know of your interest. Who knows? Somebody near or dear to you might be feeling generous.

Moving on then to the commercial markets, let us start at the bottom of the dung heap and work, not so much up, but through it.

Firstly, and hardly worth mentioning were it not to warn you most strongly against them, is anyone calling themselves 'private dealers', 'dealer collectors' or 'consultants'. They usually effect a middle initial so that Bill Smith on their card becomes William J. Smith. The first two obviously do not know what they really are and the third reminds me of the castrated tom cat who, being incapable of practising, became a consultant. All three should be avoided at all costs.

Next is the boot sale, of which very little can be said in its favour from the point of view of antiques collecting. Having heard numerous tales of the wonderful finds to be had at these events, I challenged the people who I knew habitually attended them to show me the purchases they had made. Not one could, but they all knew someone who had.

I decided to run an experiment. If people with no great knowledge and very little capital were getting lucky at boot sales, then I, with a fair amount of knowledge and plenty of capital, should make a killing. On Saturday nights I would scan the local rag, carefully noting the location of the various sales, then plotting a route which would enable me on Sunday morning to visit as many as possible. Seven o'clock each Sunday saw me on the road and going to as many as four or five sales. I kept this up for four months and many an item I bought for a pound or so which was worth five or six in the shop, sometimes several in one morning, sometimes none at all.

Once, I met a guy who was genuinely clearing his house because he was moving and spent a couple of hundred quid, the biggest purchase I ever made. I never once saw a single item of any merit. At the end of the four months hard labour I calculated the rewards, which amounted on average to the princely sum of £22.50 per morning, not counting the cost of my petrol.

When I recounted this experiment to a gentleman who I knew to be an avid boot sale fan, he gave me a very different point of view. While he fully agreed with me, he felt that given the choice of mowing the lawn, helping with the Sunday lunch or entertaining the in-laws, he would readily pay £25 a morning to get out of the house.

I really should have had more sense than to try the experiment, as I know full well that on the very rare occasions that boot sale dealers do get anything worthwhile, they invariably pick the brains of proper dealers before putting it on their stall.

Actually, I'll let you into a little secret where this can work in your favour. When a real dealer cottons onto the fact that one of these 'boot sale bandits' is constantly picking his brains, the dealers' revenge system comes in to play. The bandit is offered £30 for an item, which he then marks up at £50 on his stall, eventually taking £40. Having made an extra £10, he thinks he has been clever. It is only when he later finds out that the item concerned was worth several hundred pounds that he realises that he was not as clever as he thought, especially if he also learns that the guy whose brains he has been picking has sent a buddy down to buy it. Unless, of course, you get there first.

The widow of one of my staff told me a rather interesting story about the boot sale brigade. Having cleared the house of all the good stuff, she decided to take a stall at a boot sale to dispose of the rest. By profession, the lady was a claims officer at the local DSS. When I met her later and asked how the boot sale had gone, she informed me that it had been a great success but an even greater embarrassment as most of the other stallholders who were there full-time were claimants of hers. I wonder how many stopped claiming the following week.

Anyone found with stolen goods in the old days claimed that they had 'fallen off the back of a lorry' or that they had bought them in a pub. These days it's 'I bought them at a boot sale', which is in fact very likely since boot sales are now the normal method of disposing of stolen goods. Please be very careful. You would not like to show your latest acquisition to your friendly dealer, only to be told that it was on last week's police stolen list. Remember also that if you go back to complain, the guy who sold it to you is unlikely to be there.

One point that might surprise you is that many of the stallholders actually buy their legitimate stock from dealers like me. They come in on Friday afternoons: 'Got any crapalata for me stall this weekend, Mr Rothery?' And I let them have boxfuls of dross left over from various deals which I am too embarrassed to put into the shop. They then sell it at highly inflated prices and come back for more the following week.

Come on now, you're not thinking there is anything good in those boxes, are you?

In fairness, it should be said that young mums who get extra clothing for the kids at reasonable prices and young couples setting up home on limited budgets find boot sales useful. The nicest thing I have found is people who have large gardens or allotments and sell their surplus produce which for quality and price beats any supermarket.

To sum up then, unless it's an excuse to get out of the house, buy some clothes for the kids or stock up on seasonal vegetables, the boot sale is unlikely to prove a very productive hunting ground for the serious antiques collector.

Moving up a very small step, we come to the fairs. These subdivide into a number of levels. Firstly, the church hall one-off event held in aid of the organ fund or the Boy Scout troop. These are not, as a rule, very productive but a pleasant way to spend a wet summer's afternoon, if only for the excellent teas laid on by the ladies of the parish, plus of course the outside chance of finding something.

Next are the regular antiques fairs, once a month in your local 'Hotel Plastico' and run by 'Arty Farty Fairs', which is probably a name dreamed up by a local businessman's wife who thought it would give her something to do and be rather fun to run an antiques fair. This probably also explains why most of the stallholders are of the same ilk: bored or greedy, or both, housewives playing at being dealers. They all meet up at the weekend to compare notes, exchange gossip and talk a lot of twaddle in what they fondly believe to be 'dealer-speak'. 'The blue rinse brigade' as the real trade knows them.

If you can put up with their long-winded lectures on every bit of tat as if it were the crown jewels and you are collecting small pieces of china or silver, they are not a bad bet, especially if you have done your homework and know your subject. Their knowledge tends to be rather shallow and, while their prices are usually high, they do think that haggling is the norm. One only has to pause and glance at an item on their stall whereupon they will take a deep breath, inflate their bosoms and give you a verbatim description of the item that they looked up last night in *Antiques for Beginners*. They then tell you that it's marked up at £50 but you can have it for £40. And all of this before you have even opened your mouth. It makes you wonder why the silly woman marked it at £50 in the first place.

One side advantage of these fairs is that if you meant to buy something but didn't, don't worry: next month they will be playing dealers at the other 'Hotel Plastico' 20 miles up the road and you can catch up with the same people, probably with the same stock, there.

Specialist fairs are very much in the same mould: part-time dealers or collectors with a smattering of professionals. Quite interesting if it's your specialty, but beware of the so-called expertise of most of these people. One 'specialist dealer' at a militaria fair was a chap who only six months before had come into my shop to buy a book on German items because he was thinking of collecting them. Now, at the militaria fair, he was an expert. I happen to know that for the rest of the week he was a builder (see later in this chapter).

'Yes, they were his boots when he was a boy'

64

One advantage of these shows is that, for some strange reason, books always seem to be cheap.

At the risk of repeating myself, I must warn you that you should never try to learn at these fairs. The so-called experts are anything but expert and have a terrible habit of inventing the answer to a question if they do not know it. These answers are known in the trade proper as 'fair fantasies'.

Moving up yet another step, we come to the more professional fairs held a couple of times a year at the local stately home. Here, the dealers tend to be either full-time stallholders or proper shopkeepers who do the occasional weekend fair. They tend to know what they are doing so it is unlikely that you will find any bargains but you will see a better standard of stock and any information you get will be much more reliable.

Lastly, we come to the super fairs, which have more than a touch of the social event about them and are held at posh venues such as Chelsea Barracks, Earl's Court and Olympia. Now here you really will see top-notch exhibits and meet highly professional dealers, but at a price. One lady exhibitor told me that to show at these events cost her overall about £20,000, a sum which had to be recovered in addition to her normal profits.

I really do not know whether to advise you to take a gold card and a chequebook or to leave both of them at home. One point that I might make is that very few professional dealers go to any of these fairs with a view to *buying* stock.

Here are a few tips to help you assess the credibility of any of the dealers you might meet at these events. If the card that you are given has only a phone number on it, ask yourself why the person is shy of giving their address. Any card that has what is obviously a private address should be treated with great caution, as indeed should any, which tell you to phone after six in the evening. This probably means the dealer is at their proper job during the day.

Do not be afraid when you meet someone who claims to be a dealer to ask them what sort of dealer they are. Are they full-time? Where is their place of business? What is their VAT number? If they tell you they are full-time but cannot afford the overheads of a shop, or that their turnover is not great enough to register for VAT, then they are obviously not in a very substantial way of business and possibly only on the fringe of the trade, with all the risks this entails for the collector.

Whenever complaints are made to the police or to professional bodies that some unsuspecting member of the public has been seen off by a wicked dealer who has made off with their money or goods or both, in 90 per cent of cases the villain of the piece invariably turns out to be a part-timer operating out of his or her back room.

The other major risk that the collector faces when buying from the part-time dealer is that of inadvertently buying stolen goods, which the vendor probably does not know are stolen. The police are usually very good when it comes to tracing stolen property. As soon as something is reported missing they contact all the specialist shops with a list and description of the goods. Most shops are more than happy to liaise with the police and, as a result, a fair quantity of goods is recovered and returned to the rightful owners and a few villains are caught.

The problem then lies in the fact that, since the part-time dealer has no registered premises and makes very sure that no one in authority knows that they are dealers, the police are unable to advise them of any stolen goods which might be in circulation. These people in their greed buy anything that is offered to them and then sell the goods on without knowing, or I suspect caring, that they are stolen.

A point to bear in mind is that, should you have the misfortune to be the victim of a burglary, then it might well be that the goods offered by the part-time dealer at these fairs are yours.

Not one in a hundred of these types ever become legitimate dealers and they invariably eventually vanish into thin air.

When later the poor old collector finds out that some of their favourite pieces are stolen, they end up losing both their goods and their money with no redress to the guy they bought them from who, by now, has found a more lucrative fiddle and disappeared into the mist.

Again I make the point, if you stick to the established dealers with proper premises, should they make a mistake and unknowingly sell you a stolen item they will very quickly put the matter right.

Somewhere between the fairs and the legitimate trade there has, in recent years, appeared a proliferation of 'arcades'. A large building has been taken over by an entrepreneur and split into booths or cabinets that are let out, I suppose by the square foot, on a weekly basis to a sub-cult of the 'blue rinse brigade'. The area rented can be as little as a shelf in a cabinet but enough for the 'trade groupie' tenant not only to claim to be 'trade' but 'trade with retail premises'.

Any collector visiting these places will find the same rank amateurism that prevails at the bottom end of the fair market. Rarely in these places can one find the person from whose stall one wishes to buy an item on display. When asked, the 'minder' in attendance usually fields any enquiry with, 'I'm afraid that's not mine. You will have to ask Mabel and she only comes in on Saturdays.' Not a lot of good if you want to buy something there and then.

If you do visit these places on Saturday, most of the booth holders are in attendance, as, I suppose, they do not have to go into work that day. I repeat what I said about fairs. It's the same in arcades. They are all right *if* you know your stuff and you are collecting *small* items of china or silver etc.

The latest in-word among this lot is to describe their stock as 'smalls', which I always thought was something to do with ladies' underwear. I rather think a better word to describe both the dealers and their stock should be 'twees'.

One Sunday morning, I made myself look smart and put a couple of gold credit cards, two chequebooks and a lot of cash in my pockets: total purchasing potential of about £200,000. Not that I was contemplating spending that much, but I was going to buy a Masonic jewel and an Egyptian army presentation piece from the silver lady and, hopefully, find some pictures for the house, plus anything else that took my fancy.

Thus equipped, I arrived at the town hall and took out a trade card to show my credentials. I had hardly got through the door when my way was barred by a fat lady smelling of body odour and cheap scent who, completely ignoring the proffered trade card, snarled at me, 'We're not open 'til eleven, you'll have to come back later.' I glanced at my watch, which showed four minutes to eleven. I was about to ask if I could wait in the foyer but, before I could do so, she bore down on me, muttering something about 'Please yerself'. No, you are quite right, I didn't go in, which was a pity because I knew that inside, among the trade groupies, there were some very good and professional dealers with whom I was hoping to do business.

This story illustrates the crass amateurism of some of the people who run these shows. No organisation with an ounce of professionalism would have allowed that woman anywhere near the public, let alone put her on the door. We cannot help asking ourselves how many more potential buyers she put off, much to the cost of the exhibitors.

'Why do you dislike the part-time dealers so much? Surely they are only people trying to make a few quid with which to improve their collections?' I am often asked this question and, recently, was asked it by a person who himself personifies all that is found objectionable by the professional dealers, regardless of what area of collecting they are dealing in, be it furniture, painting, jewellery or, as in my case, militaria. This person is a classic case of the part-time dealer. He first came to my notice when six months or so ago he came into the shop and expressed an interest in collecting German items of the post-1920s era. He sought advice and guidance as to what books he should buy to learn about the subject. He was shown courtesy and given good, honest advice and sold some books at a slightly discounted price to help him get started.

The gentleman was by profession a highly reputable builder with an established business and enjoyed a good standard of living. Imagine, if you will, our horror when one of our good steady customers came in with an item that we had recently sold him and demanded his money back as the item was a fake. This was the first complaint of any sort that we had had for seven years. The item was minutely examined and no fault could be found, so the client was asked on what grounds he based his complaint.

He informed us that the item had been subjected to ultra-violet light and showed signs of man-made materials that were not available in the late 1920s, early 1930s and, therefore it must be a fake. Asked how he knew all this, he informed us that a dealer had told him. When pressed, he admitted that it was at a militaria fair and the dealer concerned was, in fact, our chum the builder who was now taking a table at these fairs and purporting to be an expert on the subject.

We went to great lengths to explain that this was a classic case of shallow knowledge. Although it was true that these materials were unheard of in the 1920s and early 1930s, they were in common use when this particular item was made in the 1940s and the item was anything but a fake. The guy's mind had now been poisoned to the item and, while he accepted our explanation, he was still not happy so, as a courtesy, we changed it. At the same time, we advised him that we were never in the future going to be the slightest bit interested in the builder's, or any other part-time expert's opinion.

The builder came in shortly after these events and was

robustly challenged about what had occurred. At the same time, equally robustly, he was appraised of the dangers of shallow knowledge. To our surprise, he immediately admitted that he had since learnt that all we had said was true and apologised profusely for the misunderstanding and embarrassment he had caused.

As a sop to our indignation, he purchased – after careful examination with the aid of a magnifying glass – a badge. Before the day was out, we received a phone call from him to the effect that, on careful examination, he was unhappy with the badge and was bringing it back tomorrow. His reception the next day was, to say the least, less than warm. Asked what he thought was wrong with the badge, his reply was, 'Well, I'm just not happy that it's right.' We changed the badge, which incidentally one of the top dealers was completely happy with and bought two days later.

We were now in the invidious position after not having had a single complaint in seven years of having two in a fortnight, both the result of a builder that played at being a dealer at weekends.

I swear this is true: before he left after exchanging the badge, he asked me, 'Mr Rothery, why have you got such a down on part-time dealers?'

It is alleged that not only do I have a short fuse and do not suffer fools gladly, but that my language can, on occasion, be somewhat colourful. The gentleman concerned would agree.

The eventual conclusion was that he, as a professional builder, most certainly abhorred the antics of cowboy builders and the disrepute they brought upon his industry. We feel equally strongly about the cowboy dealers that inhabit the fairs and who bring disrepute on our industry. The above is not a one-off. It is happening all day, every day, in every field of collecting.

Not satisfied with leaving the professional dealers to clear up the mess and mayhem that these people cause, there are other matters to address. All businessmen and women accept that, much as they could do without it, competition is a fact of life and probably not a bad thing in a free society. Hence, they can put up with their fellow traders who pay the same business rates, taxes and VAT, business people who are subject to all the same petty regulations to which they must comply, no matter how onerous. They are not at all happy with people who compete with them at weekends, but do not have the overheads and not one in a hundred of whom pay a penny in tax or VAT on their ill-gotten gains. They are, in fact, seriously pissed off with them and long for the day when the DSS, Customs and Excise and the Inland Revenue descend on them and sort them out.

You now perhaps have some inkling as to why I and other businessmen and women are not greatly enamoured of the weekend dealer.

We now come to what is, in all likelihood, going to prove to be your most productive area of both collectables and knowledge: the antiques shop. As with the fairs and auctions, these come in many forms and guises. Let me see if I can put them in some sort of order and evaluate the different types.

The word 'junk' is not one that I like, remembering as I do some good advice given to me by a very wise old dealer who said, 'Always remember, Rothery, that what you are referring to as junk is probably someone else's pride and joy. They may not have much, so please do not take away from them either their pride or their joy.'

It is, however, a word much used when describing the lower end of the market; the junk shop and the house clearer are very much one and the same. They get whatever is left over after the family has looted the late Uncle Bill's house and the person from the auctions has gone through to see if anything is worth putting in the next sale. Only then will the family solicitor call in the house clearer to take away the dross.

Very occasionally some worthwhile item is overlooked and the house clearer gets a victory, or 'tickle' as they call it: but don't think that it will be discovered by you. House clearers may not be at the posh end of the trade but they are not daft. They usually recognise quality when they see it and any bits of worth are taken to their favourite buyer in that field: silver to the silver people, pictures to the picture people and so on.

The chances of any item passing through this chain and ending up in a 50p bowl are remote but it can happen – about as often as you winning the pools. If you are collecting things from the 1930s, 1940s or 1950s – old radios, records or any item that was in general use at that time – then these are the places to look because, by definition, Old Uncle Bill and his contemporaries who are now sadly dying off are the very people who had these items as everyday goods and chattels.

House clearers and junk shops are not, however, likely to prove productive if you are collecting the more traditional older antiques. In these days of specialisation, the old-fashioned general shop with stuffed bears, vintage cameras and Georgian chairs is very rare. Now, the cameras are in the camera shop, the chairs in the chair shop and the poor old Bruno is non-PC.

However, you can still find the shops which, while not as wide-ranging as the old types, specialise in several items at once. For instance, the furniture people have a wide range of furnishings including pictures, tapestries and silverware as well as chairs and tables. Collectors are mixed in their views over this specialisation. To some, they miss the variety offered by the old general shops, to others it is a lot more convenient to see a wide selection of their chosen field in one place.

So much for the theory, now to the practicalities.

Unless you are collecting something that is so obscure that you have to travel the world to find additions to your collection, I strongly advise that you keep your hunting as near to home as possible. This allows you to visit your local shops on a regular basis and to get to know them and they you. This is most important if you are to build up a good relationship with them and become one of their regulars.

Go through the Yellow Pages and visit the shops you think will be best suited to your needs. Note I say *visit* them. Do not rely on what someone else tells you about them. It is a well-known fact that, for some unknown reason, certain dealers will immediately strike sparks with one collector, yet get on like a house on fire with another. For no apparent reason the reverse also applies with the collectors and the dealers. I heard of one occasion when a collector was vilifying a dealer in a restaurant and another collector who was also dining there, hearing his favourite dealer being derogated, left his dinner, walked over to the first guy's table and laid him out cold.

Dave Crabtree and I used to discuss this strange phenomenon at great length. People would go into his shop and make derogatory remarks about me and others would do the same about him in my shop. We called them the 'Rotheryites' and the 'Crabtreeites'. We could understand why the people with whom we had fallen out might do this, but it was those who had never been in our shops, let alone met us, that confused us. We often wondered if they thought they were building up brownie points by slagging off the competition. The answer then is, regardless of what you hear, go and look at the various dealers and make up your own mind.

I have just remembered an occasion when a visitor to the shop, after enjoying a long interesting conversation, suddenly said, 'Mr Rothery, you're quite a nice guy.' I thanked him and asked what had prompted him to make that observation. I was rather taken aback when he informed me, 'I was talking to a couple of collectors the other night and they reckoned you were the biggest bastard on God's earth!'

Make a point of introducing yourself to the proprietor and his staff, have a look at the stock and get a general feel of the place. Make a few visits and find out what the house rules are: will they put things aside for you with or without a deposit? Is it cash only or will they take credit cards? Make a point of finding out how long the business has been going. If it's a long time, then common sense tells you that, were they villains, they would not have lasted that long. We can also be confident that no reputable business of many years standing is going to risk its reputation by diddling you or any other member of the public for a piddling few hundred pounds, let alone less.

If you like what you see, start trying to build a relationship, which is not always an easy thing to do as many of the older dealers can be rather eccentric and do not suffer fools gladly. But I'll tell you this: if you do get on with them, they will move heaven and earth to look after you and help you to build your collection.

Remember the old saying: 'the best restaurant in the world

is the one you are known in'. It's the same with an antiques shop. Bear in mind that your tame, friendly dealer is a professional and you stand more chance of winning the National Lottery than of getting something for nothing from them but equally they will never knowingly try to see you off. They value your goodwill far too much to risk that. If, by any chance, you think they have made a mistake or not treated you fairly, for goodness sake talk to them about it. They can hardly rectify a wrong if they are unaware of it.

All parties should remember always that the collector will never put together a decent collection without the goodwill and help of a few dealers, and the dealers will not eat without the goodwill and help of their customers. We are not enemies or competitors. We can neither of us exist without the trust and help of the other. Not to put too fine a point on it, like it or not, we need each other.

The alternative, if you do not like what you see when you visit a dealer – the air is full of pipe smoke, they will not haggle or they are rude – is to regretfully look elsewhere for a dealer with whom you feel more at ease.

Mention should be made of the posh shops at the upper end of the market. Of course, the stock in them is usually high quality, with prices to match, but again, remember the old adage 'price is what you pays, quality is what you gets', or the other version, 'if you pays peanuts, you gets monkeys'. Do not be afraid of these shops. The people in them are human just like anybody else and they are not necessarily ultra-expensive. Here is a true story, which I think illustrates the point perfectly.

Marmion Road in Southsea had a posh end and a less posh end. My own shop was in the posh end and at the other end was the establishment of a great character by the name of Skipper, who wore the most disreputable looking clothes and was followed everywhere by an equally disreputable looking dog.

Skipper's was in every sense of the word a junk shop. Each evening, he would enlist the help of any passer-by in forcing shut his shop door against a mass of old bicycles, mangles and large unidentifiable objects that were threatening to flow back onto the pavement. Each morning, his shout of warning could be heard the length of the road as he released the door to allow the same rusting mass to come crashing out onto the pavement, causing risk to life and limb to any unfortunate in the way.

It so happened that I had acquired a bundle of 100 Indian swords; nothing to write home about, but ideal for furnishing or young collectors just starting. Half the swords had leather scabbards and half had khaki cloth. The price in those days was £6 10s for the leather and £5 10s for the cloth, with 10s off if you bought more than one. The swords were displayed halfway down the shop in clear view of anyone looking in the window, as were the prices. Each Thursday evening, Skipper would purchase several of them and disappear down the road to his emporium. Saturdays, the lookers and browsers would glance briefly into my place then hurry off to the less expensive end of the road. You could have bet money that those same people would reappear past my shop with what was obviously one of the swords wrapped in newspaper under their arm and looks of smug satisfaction on their faces.

So intrigued was I by this weekly performance that I dispatched a tame collector to Skippers to find out what was going on. My spy, when he returned, could hardly contain himself as he related how he had watched Skipper carefully bury one of the swords in the depths of his junk and how the lookers and browsers had 'found' it, beaten the old boy down from £11 to £10 and left the shop over the moon with their 'bargain'. At that point, the wicked old devil had got another sword from the packing case that served as his office, and buried that in the junk ready for the next set of bargain hunters. To my total embarrassment I must tell you that, at the end of the exercise, Skipper sold 96 swords to my 4.

This is typical of the mistake so many collectors make in assuming that any goods in a half decent looking shop must, by definition, be expensive, whilst those in a junk shop must, by the same definition, be cheap. Please do not fall into that trap. Some of my best buys have been in very up-market shops, which, in my younger days, I would have been too overawed to enter. I remember asking a great hero of mine, Harry Leigh, what he thought of the way I was presenting my shop. His wise reply was, 'Very nice, but you don't want too much of a Bond Street flash or you'll frighten off the punters.'

I recall on one occasion talking to Tony Earle of Wilton, who was another very switched on dealer as well as a thoroughly nice chap. He admitted that there was one very old established and posh antiques shop in his area where, man and boy, he had looked longingly through the window but never dared enter because he was completely overawed by the grandness of the place. I told him what I have told you. Go in and ask. They are not going to eat you and they might have something in your line, which does not fit in with their general stock, and which they will sell at a reasonable price to clear it.

The next time I saw Tony, he dragged me into the back room and produced a really nice silver-mounted sword. I valued it in my mind at about £300 and, to my amazement, Tony told me that he wanted £225. I agreed but pointed out to him that he was a bit on the low side. He smiled and told me that he knew its real value but, acting on my advice, he had plucked up the courage to visit the posh shop that we had talked about. Not only had they been absolutely charming but they had sold him the sword for £200 because they did not like having swords in the shop.

'If it had not been for you telling me to visit the place, I would never have gone in there, so I reckon by rights you should share my luck. I am happy with a quick £25 profit from you, Mr Rothery, but if you don't want it, it can go into the window and any other bugger can pay £300!'

Having searched the county and located the shops, how then do we judge if they are properly and professionally run and therefore worthy of our custom and patronage? Here are a few things to look for.

The first good indication is that all the goods are clearly priced. If they are not, we have the time-consuming annoyance of having to ask how much each item is and wonder if the answer depends on the vendor's assessment of what we might pay.

Some dealers give a brief description and date on the price tag and I am sure they try to be as accurate and helpful as possible in this. Personally, I do not follow this practice, as I firmly believe that most collectors prefer to form their own opinion. I also feel that it is a bit patronising on the dealer's part to assume that the clients do not know what they are looking at. From my own experience I find that such descriptions tend to invite the smart arse to challenge the information. This invariably leads to an argument with an idiot who had no intention of buying the piece in the first place and only wants to show off their knowledge or, more likely, their abysmal ignorance.

Apart from the above, a plethora of signs on the door of the establishment should make you highly suspicious: 'No drinks, no food, no children, no smoking'. Whenever I see this sort of thing I cannot but wonder if I am entering the domain of some latter-day dictator who at some later date might well add, 'No Jews, no black people and no Freemasons' to his collection of 'nos'. If, on entering, we find yet more signs in the same vein, we must ask ourselves, is the management here so ineffective that they cannot run their establishment without the aid of these rather offensive epistles? In which case, can we rely on them to help us with our collection?

The same thing always crosses my mind when I am confronted with so-called humorous signs which are meant to be amusing but often verge on the obscene. All right, I suppose

'Do you buy clocks?'

in a person's study or the toilets of a work canteen such signs are ok, but do they give us confidence in an establishment where we are going to spend our hard-earned money and seek sound professional advice?

Here is some advice to the dealers on the question of signs. Our much-beloved public are either incapable of reading signs, choose to ignore them or do not believe that the signs apply to them. I watched in one shop as the proprietor, in an attempt to stop people messing up his window display, carefully fitted a piece of hardboard across the back of the window to prevent access. On the shop side of the hardboard he had written in large letters 'Please do not touch items in this window'. The first woman to come in stood back and carefully read his sign. She then attacked the board, wrenching and tugging until it gave way under her onslaught. Having gained access to the window, she picked up each and every item, then having inspected it minutely, threw it carelessly into a heap. The 'lady', having completely wrecked the poor guy's display, then departed without so much as a 'Good morning'.

A more heartwarming example of this high degree of intelligence exhibited by some collectors when faced with signs was when, during our annual sale, rather than re-price each item, we would have a 'one price window'. Goods with price tags of between £20 and £30 would be placed in the window with the original labels still on. We then plastered the window with signs saying 'All items in this window £15 each regardless of marked price'. In would come the intelligentsia of the antiques collectors' scene and, after careful examination of the items and many knowledgeable comments, they would then look at the labels and ask, 'Would you take £20 for this?' Guess what? We did! The Royal British Legion benefited each year to the tune of some £200.

Having said all that about signs, I must admit that I had a certain sympathy with one that I saw outside a church which was ideally suited to an antiques shop: 'Our job is to feed the sheep, not amuse the goats'; and another in a shop which read: 'Prices are liable to fluctuate depending on the attitude of the client'.

To sum up then, the door of a properly-run shop will have a clear indication of the opening hours and nothing more. By the way, it follows that the shop should always and without fail be open during those hours. Not to be open when they say they will is not only bad manners but bad business practice. If a shopkeeper (in antiques or any other trade) has not the courtesy to be open when they say they will be, then they most certainly do not deserve your support.

Inside, the goods should be clearly priced with possibly a short description on the labels. Another pointer to the collector as to how well the shop is run is if goods which have been sold are still on the shelf, especially if the purchaser's name is on the label. If you had bought that item, would you want the whole world to know?

One thing that is a dead giveaway to the shopkeeper's sanity is if the idiot has things on display which are not for sale. What sort of moron is it that wastes valuable selling space and upsets the customers by teasing them with goods they cannot buy? When you do have the misfortune to come across these very odd places, where the nicest pieces are marked 'Not for sale, owner's private collection', my best advice would be to give them a wide berth. The person concerned is obviously incapable of knowing whether they are running a business or a private museum.

Here's another little clue to tell us something about the expertise of the dealer. Look behind where he or she sits. There is probably a row of reference books. Now look carefully: if these are proper technical books on the various subjects it would tend to indicate that the dealer does their homework, which is to the benefit of all concerned. If, on the other hand, there are no reference books in evidence, it indicates that the dealer concerned knows, or thinks they know everything there is to know without recourse to any books. You are then in the presence of either a genius or a fool. Be very careful.

The real danger sign is if the shelf contains a whole row of out-of-date price guides and reviews; anyone who is so pig ignorant as to need these for identification, or stupid enough to use them for valuations, should be strenuously avoided.

Attitude towards pricing and haggling is another good guide as to the integrity of the dealer. If, even before you ask, they offer you something off the asking price and then allow you to bargain them down even further, you are obviously dealing with a fool. They either have no idea how to price their stock in the first place, or are desperate, for some nefarious reason, to get shot of the item as quickly as possible. You are, in all probability, paying over the odds anyway but you will also of course get an almighty ego boost, thinking that you have got a bargain. For goodness sake, use your common sense. You know perfectly well that all con men make their living by playing on the ego and greed of gullible people and I don't think you are that daft.

A better bet is when the dealer appears to have their prices pitched at about the right level and refuses to haggle or only knocks a little off the price. This shows that they know what they are doing and can't be bothered to mess about. It also shows that they have complete confidence in both their goods and their prices.

One last tip is, believe it or not, good manners and enthusiasm. If the person you are dealing with is polite and shows genuine interest in what they are selling to you, they are probably reliable and well worth you developing as one of your regular dealers.

Having given you all this advice on dealer appraisal, may I once again remind you that you are collecting for fun, so if you enjoy the cut and thrust of pitting your wits against the rough boys and girls so be it: enjoy. But promise me that when you get hurt you won't go crying to your favourite tame dealer.

Two other sources I should mention are mail order and, very similar, the internet. My own experiences of mail order, both as a dealer and a member of the public, are not the happiest. As a dealer with a shop, I found that by the time my catalogue went out, half the better items had already been sold, which did not please the people who sent for them. The items that were sold through the catalogue more often than not resulted in acrimonious correspondence regarding the descriptions in the catalogue which I thought were accurate and fair but some recipients did not. It was all very messy and I quickly stopped doing it. As a member of the public, I like to see what I am getting for my money and to be in a position to sort out the vendor if there are any problems. So even if I pay more for an item by buying locally, that's all right with me.

Antiques and collectables are not, in my opinion, the sort of things that lend themselves to mail order. Buying from the internet is something of a new innovation and, whilst I have no experience of it personally, logic tells me that the same problems will arise as with ordinary mail order.

5

The Auctions

It was once said of auctioneers that they were the world's second oldest profession without the moral standards of the world's oldest profession. Yet somehow, with the aid of various TV programmes, they have conned the public into thinking that they are the only honest brokers on the antiques scene, which is very far from the truth.

Think about it: are not most auctioneers also estate agents?

Some years ago, as a result of a long boozy dinner followed by a great many brandies, I was prevailed upon to assist a well-known auction house which was suffering from a major financial crisis. The sums of money involved were not inconsiderable, so naturally I took some equity in the firm, which gave me a seat on the board. Being basically sound, it was only a couple of years before it was back on its feet and my money was returned. At this stage, I did of course give up both my equity in the firm and my seat on the board. No complaints. I earned a modest return on my investment and the house was grateful for the help I had rendered, so we parted the best of friends and still are. The point about all this is that, during my time as a director there, I had unlimited access to every department and hence I have seen the workings of an auction house from the inside. Believe me, it was quite an eye-opener.

Let us then strip away this façade of genteel honesty and false *bonhomie* that a gullible public has been duped into thinking surrounds the auction trade and see if we can get nearer the truth.

The advertisement in the local rag tells us that the Lions, Rotary or any other worthy and hard-working organisation is running a roadshow on Friday at the town hall. It will be attended by Rupert Golightly-Smith of Sleazies, the well-known auction house, assisted by Penelope Grand-Derriere, who will, for £2 per item, value your antiques. Entry £3, all proceeds to go to charity.

An absolutely genuine and worthy promotion, properly run by hard-working volunteers who give unsparingly of their time to raise money for charity and every penny raised, I have no doubt whatsoever, will go to those charities. More strength to their elbow say I. Charity, however, is the last thing on the mind of the auction house representatives present. They are there to squeeze every last drop of publicity out of the event. They are also there to use their guiles to persuade anybody attending with a half-decent antique to place it immediately or at some future date into one of their sales. Business cards will be dispensed to all and sundry with the exhortation, 'Do contact us if you or any of your friends have anything you would like us to sell on your behalf.'

Why not indeed? They are there to whip up as much business as they can for their company and if they do not find entries for future auctions, their firm will go out of business and they will be out of a job. Why oh why then must they effect this pose that they are doing it out of the goodness of their hearts and in the interest of charity, when they are really there in their own interests, and why oh why are the public daft enough to believe them?

Let us start at the bottom of this particular heap and work our way through it. One-day auctions held in church halls and hotel rooms are usually the bright idea of one of the many 'trade groupies' who lurk around the fringe of the trade but are really only playing at it. Note again, the fancy title 'undiscovered auctions' or some other unlikely name. The guy running it, Joe Soap, becomes 'Joseph Q. Soap, Auctioneer and Valuer', according to his card. The grandiose title is probably adopted in an attempt to give himself and his enterprise a non-existent degree of credibility. The adverts say something like 'Goods brought in by 12 noon. Sale starts 2pm', which gives his wife time to type up a rough catalogue, the descriptions in all likelihood being supplied by the vendors themselves.

Ask the same questions that you would of a dealer. Where are their offices? Are they full-time, qualified auctioneers? etc. Many local dealers put goods into these events that they have got stuck with or are too embarrassed to put in their shops. They hope, of course, that some idiot will not only buy them but will get auction fever and pay over the odds for them. Make sure it's not you. My advice would be not to waste your time on this sort of event.

Most areas have an old, established estate agent who occasionally holds a house sale a couple of times a year or a general goods sale. Honest enough people, but since they do not as a rule employ a full-time cataloguer, they tend to enlist the aid of friends who they meet at Rotary lunches or the odd collector that they know for their descriptions. So do bear in mind that if you are buying on the strength of the catalogue description, it is probably only the opinion of the local bank manager or fishmonger! This can, of course, work both ways, but it's a bit of a gamble.

One local auction house had me confused for years with both its descriptions and its estimates, until I had occasion to go into the office one day. I should have guessed; there behind the desk of the chap that did the cataloguing was a row of out-of-date antiques guides. They were rubbish enough when they were first printed, let alone now they were out of date, and this poor misguided (that's a good pun) soul had been using them to write the catalogue each month. I was not sure whether I was more sorry for him or the people who had bought stuff on the strength of his descriptions.

Basically the same rules apply to auction houses as to shops. The more established and specialised the auction house is, the less the risk of losing your shirt.

Finally, we come to the so-called 'famous' auction houses, the 'Super Sleazies'. I once heard Christie's described as 'Gentlemen pretending to be auctioneers' and Sotheby's described as 'Auctioneers pretending to be gentlemen'. In my opinion, it is to be regretted that both failed in their pretensions. If you have that sort of money and are that advanced a collector, then you have in all probability passed the stage where you need my humble advice. Do bear in mind, however, that even the big boys often get things wrong and they have been known to drop the most almighty and resounding clangers.

My favourite was in a sale of old Dutch masters. The auction house had brought over the leading expert from Amsterdam to do the cataloguing and had given him a girl from the office to write down his descriptions. The catalogue duly appeared but it was too late to alter one lot, where the expert's comments on the painting had got mixed up with the artist's name. There is evidently no great old Dutch master by the name of A. Bastard!

Here, for your amusement, and perhaps as a warning, are some horror stories of my own experiences with auctioneers over the years. I do assure you that each one is the absolute truth.

On one occasion, we had sent a large number of goods to a well-known auctioneer and had a reasonably successful sale. The few unsold lots were returned to us, with the exception of a rather nice piece of French prisoner-of-war work depicting the crucifixion at Calvary which appeared to be missing. Somewhat concerned, we sent a telegram to the auction house which read, 'Reference unsold lots. Where is Calvary?'

Despite several reminders, we had no reply. Then, after some days, we received the following: 'Unsold lots should have been received last week. We believe Calvary is a hill due west of Jerusalem. Why?'

The catalogue said: 'Very rare and interesting hand-ignited arquebus found in a cave at Wivenhoe and thought to be a relic of the Monmouth rebellion'. The item so described was, in fact, the remains of a bayonet-fighting training device, clearly dated 1908.

Having been asked by a lady of my acquaintance to take four oil paintings to our local auctioneer, I arrived exactly on time for my appointment, only to be kept waiting for some 15 minutes. During this time, I read the various pamphlets and auction reports of previous sales which were lying on the waiting room table. Eventually, out came Rupert and, not even apologising for his tardiness, glanced at the paintings and informed me that they were of no merit but he would accept them as one lot as they might be of use to someone for furnishing. They would, he further informed me with some smugness, sell for about £40 the lot. Picking up one of the reports on the table, I pointed out that these paintings were almost identical in size, subject and indeed by the same local artist as those mentioned in his pamphlet, which claimed that his company had previously sold individually and at a great deal more in a previous sale. He stared for some time at the pamphlet then, completely unabashed, announced 'Oh! I didn't see that there. I suppose we will have to sell them separately.' Not only did they, but each painting sold for over £200.

On the subject of paintings, I took some portraits to one of the better-known, posh London auctioneers who, having looked at them, informed me that they were not good enough for that firm and I should take them to one of the more modest sale rooms along the road. This I did and was reasonably pleased with the results. That is until some months later, when a friend drew my attention to a catalogue from the original auctioneers who were now offering the same paintings they had refused from me in their next sale. Now then, what do you make of that?

My friend Bert was sitting at home minding his own business, when he was swooped upon by half the regional crime squad who, armed with a search warrant, were looking for some antiques stolen in a recent major robbery. They found nothing to do with the robbery in question but one bright DC with an eye for antiques spotted a collection of ivories of considerable importance. Bert was asked how he had come by them and explained that he had bought them some years before from a member of the public.

The officers took a couple of pieces as examples, which they subsequently showed to a leading expert at one of the so-called great auction houses. The expert identified the items as being of major importance, an opinion he repeated when shown the rest of the collection at a later date. The expert then added that, in his opinion, the collection was of such international importance that it could not possibly come from an ordinary member of the public and, furthermore, any dealer of Bert's experience must have known this. Despite far-reaching enquiries, no reports of the collection being stolen could be found.

Notwithstanding all this, Bert was charged with receiving property knowing it to have been stolen and, in the ensuing court case, the expert duly repeated his opinion that the ivories must have been stolen and that, as a specialist dealer, Bert must have known. Fortunately for Bert, the case received massive publicity as a result of which the original guy who sold the ivories to Bert came forward, identified the goods and confirmed Bert's story. Bert, of course, was cleared of all allegations. But that was not the end of the story. Bert's reputation had received a terrible bashing and his private life had been upset. He was also very much out of pocket, the costs he received from the court hardly covering the cost of his defence. He decided, therefore, to sell his collection of ivories and, bearing in mind what he had heard the expert say in court, felt that the best place to sell them would be the famous auction house where the expert worked. The superior young lady at reception looked down her nose at Bert and his ivories and made it perfectly clear that they were not of a suitable quality for them to consider. Bert was not happy and said so in no uncertain terms. Just before things got out of hand and Bert was about to be ejected by security, someone with a bit of common sense sent for the great man who grudgingly agreed to take the ivories for sale. They eventually came up in a specialist sale where surprise, surprise, they only made a few hundred quid. Bert was even more unhappy and consulted his solicitor. The matter was eventually settled out of court but the terms of the settlement were never made public. Suffice it to say that whenever the case comes up in conversation, Bert says nothing but a beatific smile spreads across his face!

The following story, in my opinion, is typical of the way some auction houses will go to any length in the pursuit of their own self-aggrandizement regardless of the damage they cause to other people's pride and feelings.

Private Joshua Makepiece was involved in a very famous action during the Second World War; in fact a film was made about it. For his part in the action, he was quite rightly awarded the Distinguished Conduct Medal. On his return to civilian life at the end of the war, Mr Makepiece returned to his old job and through hard work he was eventually made foreman, a position he held for many years.

During this period, he took the opportunity to purchase his council house from the local authority. The time then came for him to retire and realise a lifelong dream that he and his wife had of a bungalow with a nice garden in Surrey. The profit on the ex-council house plus his savings should provide the funds for the purchase, and his foreman's pension would give them an income for a very pleasant retirement. Unfortunately, prices had risen somewhat and he was a bit short on the purchase price.

He therefore decided to sell his medals. As he put it to me, 'Never wear the bloody things anyway.' He was prevailed upon to put it to auction and no sooner had he agreed than the auction house publicity department got to work: 'War hero forced to sell medals to buy retirement home!' shrieked *The Daily Blabber*, followed by a heart-rending and completely spurious story that our hero was facing homelessness.

When the day of the sale came, there were more journalists and TV cameras than buyers in the room. The top dealers and collectors had estimated that the medal was worth about £2,000 but with all the publicity would probably make twice that. The disbelief on their faces when the bidding passed £25,000 defies description.

This drama was, of course, caught on the TV cameras aimed at the podium and at the very large logo of the auction house behind the podium. The papers the next day were full of it, together with a picture of Mr Makepiece sat in the front row of seats in the auction room. It was said that when asked for his reaction he was speechless, which in view of the amount of 'hospitality' that the publicity people had poured down his throat was not surprising!

'What idiot paid that?' we all asked. Nobody among the audience had even got to bid. The identity of the mystery buyer and which institution he or she had escaped from was a major topic of conversation for some weeks. Then, like all news, interest faded until, lo and behold, more headlines: 'War hero gets his medals back: today, a spokeswoman for Sleazies announced that the medals of Private Makepiece featured in their recent sale had been bought by the auction house and were to be returned to him. Mr Makepiece was not available at his home in Surrey to comment.'

No. As a matter of fact, he was having a drink with me!

What a lovely heartwarming story. The old boy got his

bungalow and his medals back. It must have cost Sleazies a fortune. I really do hate to disillusion you. True, he got both the bungalow and his medals back but the fact of the matter is that it was not an idiot who paid out all that money, but a very shrewd publicist working for the auctioneers. The whole thing was no more than a cold-blooded publicity stunt where, for a trifling £25,000, the auctioneers got about £500,000 worth of publicity. No genuine bids were taken in the room that day. The figure had been decided long before the sale, as had the arrangements to squeeze the maximum amount of publicity out of the whole operation.

As a result of these events, dozens of other DCM holders, many in dire straits, put their own medals into auction. The fact that few of them made as much as £1,000 was not publicised. Nor was their bitter disappointment.

At the end of that drink I was having with Mr Makepiece, when he was not available for comment, I asked him how he felt now that it was all over. I print his answer in full with no apologies.

'Well, I didn't want all that publicity and the Old Woman was pretty upset and embarrassed by it all. And then, of course, everyone thought I was well off and expected me to buy them drinks down the British Legion, so I had to stop going there which I miss. I'll tell you one thing, Mr Rothery. All those posh people at Sleazies might talk and act like a load of poofters, but they are as hard and as cunning as the buggers I was fighting when I got that gong.'

The gentleman concerned will no doubt recognise this story even though I have changed his name to avoid any further embarrassment to him or his wife. If you are reading this, 'Mr Makepiece', I salute you sir.

One rather odd situation concerning the public and auctions arose at my old shop. I am not sure that I completely understand it even now. In the next street was an auction room and a chap from there used to come round periodically to ask me if I had anything for the next sale. I would let him take a few items that had been hanging around the shop for too long or that I wanted to be rid of for some reason. The amazing thing was that these items invariably made 20 to 30 per cent more than I had been asking in the shop. In those days the commission was a straight 10 per cent, no VAT and no unsold commission, so I was quite happy with the situation. What was more amazing was that the people paying all this extra money had seen these goods in my shop at considerably less, yet seemed perfectly happy to go to the auction and pay higher prices.

I asked one gentleman, who I knew did this on a regular basis, why he did it. His explanation puzzles me to this day: 'Well, Mr Rothery, you have always told me that you, as the proprietor of this establishment, are the sole arbiter as to what the prices will be in your shop. But, you recognise the right of the collector not to pay those prices if they do not agree with you, which is perfectly right and proper. However, sometimes you have things that I rather fancy but do not buy because, with due respect, I only have your opinion as to their worth. When I see these same articles at the auction, I am perfectly happy to pay as much as 40 per cent more because at auction I know it is an open market. The items are fetching their true value rather than the one you have arbitrarily put on them. To me, it is worth the extra 40 per cent to know that.'

Charity auctions should also be mentioned. It is another odd situation where mostly the prices are sky high for no other reason than that most of the bidders want to appear to be generous and (maybe rightly) such auctions raise amounts of money far beyond the true value of the lots. It should be said, however, that I have seen some superb items donated so, if you fall in love with something and do pay a bit over the odds, what does it matter if it's in a good cause? It is unlikely in the extreme that you will pick up any bargains at these events.

Among those things that no one seems to read are the

conditions of sale, which all auctioneers impose. It should be said, in all fairness, that these conditions are displayed around the salerooms, are available from the office and are printed inside every catalogue. All well and good if they made any sense and were in fact applicable in law, which of course they have been proved not to be in numerous recent cases. Notwithstanding the fact that these conditions of sale have been successfully challenged in the courts, the auction houses still insist on publishing them. The reason for this, in my opinion, is that if some mild mannered member of the public complains, their attention is quickly and forcibly drawn to the conditions of sale. It is only when some more switched on person tells them that they are prepared to argue the matter in court that the auctioneers immediately cave in and settle as quickly and quietly as possible.

One monumental bit of gobbledegook I found among the conditions stated that, 'Responsibility for the lot passes to the purchaser on the fall of the hammer'. Does this mean then that having successfully bid £20,000 for a piece of Meissen, if the porter drops it as a result of one too many beers at lunchtime, I am responsible?

The next condition further confounds the situation: 'Ownership of the lot will not pass to the purchaser until payment for the lot has been made in full'. According to the auctioneer's conditions, we now have a situation where £20,000 worth of Meissen is smashed to smithereens by a befuddled auction house employee and it is the purchaser's responsibility even though they do not own it. I would rather like to see that argued in court.

Whilst we are on the subject of auction house terms and conditions, try this little scenario. Having nothing better to do of a Sunday and being in a mildly masochistic mood, we watch that well-known ongoing advertisement for the auction trade, *The Antiques Roadshow*. This week's 'experts' are our old friends R. Golightly-Smith Esq. and Ms Penelope Grande-

Derriere. With great skill and expertise, they immediately identify every item shown to them and give us an in-depth history of its background. When? Where? How was it made? By whom? And finally, what it's worth – 'in auction' of course.

On the strength of this *bravura* display of in-depth knowledge and expertise, we then take our family treasure to Sleazies, the well-known auction house where the pair of them work. Before accepting our treasure, our attention is drawn to the terms and conditions including one which tells us, 'The company accepts no responsibility for the accuracy, condition or dates contained in any lot description'. What a very strange disclaimer for people who, on Sunday, were telling several million TV viewers of their wide-ranging and infallible expertise.

Those thinking of employing the services of an auction house should also consider the question of what it is going to cost. The purchaser is buying in competition so, by definition, they will pay more than anyone else in the room is willing to pay for that item. Having done so, they will then be required to pay a further buyer's commission of between 10 and 15 per cent, which may or may not include VAT. Add to this the cost of travel to the auction and our bargain gets to be anything but.

The poor old vendor is in for even more of a shock. Having been informed that the commission is 12 or 15 per cent, they are more than a little surprised at all the additional charges such as insurance, illustrations etc. Some cheeky devils actually charge for cataloguing. In the event of the item not selling, you might well be charged unsold commission plus storage. Should you change your mind and withdraw an item, you will be charged a withdrawal fee. On top of all of these hidden charges, which will probably not be drawn to your attention when you enter an item, you will of course pay VAT.

The fact is that anyone selling at auction is lucky if they

actually get back 80 per cent of the selling price but, more likely, it will be 70 or 75 per cent of the hammer price.

To sum up from a buyer's point of view, buying at auction is, as a rule, an expensive way of building a collection. They do, however, tend to get the rarer objects and a wider choice. Hence, if they have something that you have been looking for for years, if you want it enough, price has to become secondary.

From the seller's point of view, if you discover that you have a very rare piece which you thought was valueless and it makes £10,000, even if after commission etc. you only get back £7,000 you will, no doubt, still be a happy bunny. The problem is when selling the more average item for which your local dealer has offered you £500. When it makes £650 in auction and months later you get a cheque from the auction house for £475, then you will not be the happiest of bunnies!

Some of my clients have been big enough and kind enough to tell me when this has happened and ruefully admitted that they wished they had listened to me in the first place. I have a pile of auction settlement statements that they have been generous enough to give me to use when persuading other clients not to make the same mistakes.

Before leaving the subject, I would mention a lady who, after waiting many months, actually got back exactly two thirds of what her goods sold for. And a gentleman who, when selling a small collection of very pretty porcelain, was persuaded by the auctioneers to have it all illustrated. He finally received £800 for a collection that sold for £1,800.

Let me spell out a simple sum on a lot selling for £1,000. The auctioneer can get £250 from the vendor and £175 from the buyer – a total of £425. Am I in the wrong business, I ask myself?

A few points on the subject of auctions before moving on to more pleasant matters.

I am always being asked by clients whether I buy my stock

from auctions. The answer is that I and other established dealers very rarely do. In the old days, it was true that most buyers at auction were dealers, but now the majority of people attending auctions are members of the public with a smattering of the fringe fraternity of the trade. There used to be a misconceived theory among collectors that if at auction you went one bid more than the dealer then you were doing all right. These days, were you to do that, the chances are that the dealer you keep outbidding is, in fact, a member of the public who is doing the same to you.

No doubt you have heard horror stories of 'The Ring', where dealers have one person bidding for stuff, then knock

'Oh him, he's from "Sleazies" the auctioneers'

the items out among themselves in the pub afterwards with the profit between the hammer price and the real value being shared between the members of the Ring. This was certainly prevalent years ago but now, due to the large numbers of the public attending auctions, the practice hardly exists. The nearest thing today might be for two dealers who are friends to agree beforehand not to bid against each other on certain items.

One point that might interest you is the fact that probably 50 per cent of goods at auction are put there by dealers of one sort or another. Personally, although I am not enamoured with auctioneers, I have probably sold a couple of hundred times more items in auctions than I have bought. There exists a type of dealer who makes a very good living buying and selling from one auction to another.

The only real danger to the beginner is the less scrupulous dealer who puts stuff into a sale and attends for the purpose of bidding his or her lots up to the reserve that they want. Having spotted a novice, it is not unknown for them to run the poor innocent up to a price well beyond that which they would originally have been satisfied with. Once again, beware auction fever.

Auctions can provide a lot of fun if you are a bit of a gambler and you have plenty of time to kill. Being there on viewing day and then having to go back on sale day, plus the travelling can indeed be time consuming but against that there is always the chance that in the 'speculative lot' or box of odds and sods there is the occasional little treasure. The results on sale day can vary a great deal depending on who is there and what they are after. You could sometimes get lucky if you are the only person there with an interest in a particular item, and make a minor killing.

6

The Law and the Collector

This is not a subject, I should imagine, that the average collector has given much thought to, but it has been shown to me
several times recently just how ignorant most collectors are on
legal matters affecting collectors and collecting.

'Ignorance of the law is no defence'. We have all heard it
said many times, but have we ever thought about it?

Talking to a client recently who I have known for many
years as a pistol collector, I was stunned to learn that he had
virtually no knowledge of the laws on firearms and relied
always on what he was told by fellow collectors and dealers
at fairs and suchlike. Apart from the police-registered firearms
dealers who are required by law to know the various acts, it
would appear from what he told me that his friends and the
dealers at the militaria fairs know even less than he does. I
should not really have been all that surprised because, on the
rare occasions that I have visited general fairs and the even
rarer occasions that I have visited militaria fairs, I have invariably seen a blatant disregard for any of the relevant laws or
regulations. The word 'anarchy' springs to mind.

At one fair, the stallholder was offering some powder flasks
and explaining with great delight that the powder was still in
them, apparently cheerfully oblivious of the fact that he could
have faced charges under the Explosives Act for possession
of explosives: offering explosives for sale to an unqualified
person, failing to keep explosives in the correct manner and

selling explosives from premises not licensed for the purpose to name but a few, and that is not to mention breaches of the fire regulations, etc.

Another stall was offering a collection of birds' eggs in contravention of the Wildlife Act, which would also have something to say about the stuffed birds on several other stalls.

The jewellery lady was selling British coins made into jewellery and next to her were a couple doing enamel work on the same type of coins. Both were possibly liable to charges of defacing coins of the realm. Talking of coins, the numismatist was offering counterfeit coins as curios, and copy medals. The charge, and this would include anyone who had bought them, would be being in possession of counterfeit currency, and carries not only heavy fines and imprisonment but still allows deportation to the colonies!

Ivory artefacts of recent manufacture, banned by international law to protect endangered species, were on show, as well as a German parachutist knife and a modern swordstick, both proscribed by the Criminal Justice Act.

The buildings used by such fairs very rarely have retail planning permission and I doubt if the organisers have even heard of public liability insurance. My guess was that over half the stallholders were in grave danger of being charged with making false unemployment benefit claims.

Let us pass swiftly over the catering facilities and regulations concerning hygiene!

If you are of the opinion that the laws of the land in no way concern the collector, do not bother with the rest of this chapter. If you are interested in how those laws affect you, the collector, read on.

At dinner one night, the conversation came round to collecting and dealers. I was horrified when my hostess, a lady whom I both respect and admire, cheerfully admitted that she always told antiques dealers that she was 'trade' in the hope of getting a discount. The rest of the party then joined in and recounted with some pride a catalogue of dirty tricks that they had all employed to cheat various dealers.

Mine hostess, who had a rather odd sense of humour, or maybe one drink too many, asked me whether, as a professional dealer, did I not think that the assembled guests had all been rather clever? I took great pleasure in explaining to them that they had all in fact committed criminal acts. They had laid themselves open to a charge of 'gaining a pecuniary advantage by means of a trick other than fraud', and had the dealers concerned chosen to report them, they could have faced not only considerable embarrassment but large fines and possibly a custodial sentence. Which, to my mind, was far from being clever. I also expressed the hope that the dealers concerned had banned her guests from their shops.

Mention of dealers banning people surprised them and I had to explain that, as with many members of the public, they were not apparently aware that even shopkeepers have rights. Not only can they ban people from their premises, but they can reserve the right of entry, ask people who are being obnoxious to leave their premises and use reasonable force to eject them if they do not do so.

By now, having the bit firmly between my teeth, I took further pleasure in explaining that not only did the dealer not have to haggle but he or she had the right to refuse to sell the item even at full price, or indeed to increase the price if he or she felt like it. They were not at all happy when I pointed out that if a dealer offered a price for an item and the vendor went away to 'think about it' or, more likely, to see if they could get 50p more elsewhere, the dealer was under no obligation to honour the offer if the vendor returned at a later date.

They all then voiced the opinion that if any dealer did any such thing to them they would never go to that shop again. To which, of course, the answer was that, if they behaved in the way they had been boasting about, the dealer would be delighted to hear it.

The party broke up soon after that and the hostess has never asked me back, thankfully.

Another small point of civil law concerns the reservation of goods against a deposit. If the purchaser fails to collect the item in the agreed time, not only can the vendor sell the goods and keep the deposit, but they could proceed against the purchaser for breach of contract. A tip here for the dealer. When you accept a deposit, put the completion date on the receipt, i.e. 'Received £20 deposit, balance of £80 to be paid by 32/13/05 and goods collected by that date'. If you do not put a completion date, it may be argued that it is an open-ended agreement and the purchaser could keep you waiting for ages for the balance and expect you to store the item for years, having paid the balance.

With regards to stolen goods, title or legal ownership of stolen goods remains, in most cases, with the person from whom they were originally stolen, regardless of how many hands they have passed through in the intervening time. The exception to this may be when an insurance claim has been paid by the insurance company to the person who lost the goods, in which case the recovered goods would be the property of the company that paid out on the claim (see also Chapter 9).

There is one piece of legislation that I personally would like to see put on the statute books and that is a law to protect dealers from dear little old ladies!

All this talk of law is very interesting but need not concern you too much, dear reader, because being the honest and decent type you are, you would never allow yourself to get into these situations in the first place.

7

Fakes, Reproductions and Other Strange Beasts

Tread carefully, dear reader. We are about to enter a minefield.

Many years ago, I had in the shop a very old and very beautiful Japanese sword which appeared to have been made about the year AD 1100. There was, among the local collectors and 'experts' much speculation as to its authenticity, so, being in no great hurry to sell it, I put it high up on the rack where the 'lookers' could not get their hands on it.

One day, I was visited by three Japanese gentlemen, one of whom explained that he was the interpreter for the other two who were professors from one of the great Japanese national museums, over here for a conference. Having heard of my sword, they had come down to Portsmouth in the hope that I would allow them to inspect it, which of course, I did.

There followed a long debate between the two old boys, which sounded as if it was getting more and more heated. Not wishing for a geriatric punch-up in my shop, I asked the interpreter what it was about. He explained to me that one old gent was quite sure that the sword was 900 years old and by a famous maker, while the other was equally adamant that it was only 850 years old and a copy with a forged signature. I asked, through the interpreter, if it really mattered, as it was a lovely old sword and all the more interesting because of the mystery surrounding it. At this, the two professors turned on me and gave me what was evidently a thorough dressing down in Japanese. Did you know that 'philistine' is the same in both languages?

Now, dear reader, what should we call this sword? Is it a fake, a reproduction or a copy? This illustrates the confusion that exists with both dealers and collectors as to which is which. So I am going to try to define the various expressions and their meaning for you. Do please bear in mind that this is only my personal interpretation.

Reproductions and copies

For simplicity let us treat these as one and the same thing. These are objects which are made in the style of antiques or curios for people who cannot afford the originals, and they are priced accordingly. There is no intention by the maker to deceive or defraud. Examples include china, furniture and a multitude of other items.

Now for some unknown reason, many collectors seem to think that all reproductions were made last week, which is most certainly not the case. When, in Victorian times, Sir Walter Scott was writing his novels about the heroes of old and our own dear queen moved into Balmoral, all things Gothic became fashionable. The *nouveau riche* of the time built huge reproduction houses and castles. They then decorated and furnished them with reproduction Elizabethan furniture and copies of old masters. Now, when those copies were made, they were well made. Italian and other foreign artisans were imported to do the work that the local tradesmen were not skilled at; time and money were of no object. With the passing of a hundred years or so, these items have acquired the marks of everyday use and the patina that only comes with age. It now takes a very shrewd person to tell the difference between the original and the Victorian copy.

Many is the time that I have heard very experienced dealers say: 'Well, it's either an original or a very good, old copy but it's a lovely piece and well worth the money.'

Most reproductions that were made last week stick out like a sore thumb, even when attempts have been made to age them.

The major problem with reproductions is when they have passed through several hands and gained a used look. Then somebody buys them thinking they have found an original and sells them on quite genuinely believing that to be the case. Unfortunately, they rarely listen when told of their mistake. I get this a lot when an item is brought into the shop by a person who is quite convinced that they know what they have got but needs to be assured that they are right. If I tell them what they want to hear, as they go out they say to whoever is with them, 'What a nice old boy, he really knows his stuff.' If I tell them what they do not want to hear, they say, 'Daft bastard, doesn't know what he's talking about.'

If you are at all worried that you might make a mistake, then fall back on the common sense approach. Any reputable dealer will, if asked, tell you exactly what the thing they are selling you is, and they will also tell you if they have any doubts about it. Do not make the mistake of buying an item which you have seen in various places at £500 for £100, then go back to the dealer and cry that you thought it was an original and not a reproduction. This is tantamount to saying to them, 'I thought you were an idiot selling a £500 item for £100 and now I know you are not, I want my money back.' For goodness sake, stop trying to be clever and talk to the dealer.

There are, among the collecting fraternity, rather silly, greedy people who expect a cast-iron guarantee of authenticity at a reproduction price.

You could, of course, chance your arm if you think you have spotted a mistake that the dealer has made, and you might get lucky. But you stand a better chance of winning the National Lottery. You surely would not have the bare faced cheek to take it back if you were wrong. Would you?

Attitudes towards reproductions and copies vary greatly

among collectors and I must admit to being a little confused by their approach to the subject. I recall on one occasion two guys in the shop looking at a certain item. One of them threw it scornfully back on the counter with the comment, 'That's only a reproduction.' The other picked it up and, after careful inspection, countered, 'Yes, but you or I could not make anything as good and we can't afford an original so I'll take it.'

This illustrates a rather odd idea that some collectors have that if they are lusting for an item far beyond their financial abilities, they believe that one day they are going to find a mad dealer who is going to sell them one for peanuts or they are going to win the pools. When offered a good reproduction of that item they refuse, saying they would rather wait for a real one. Presumably they then go through life in a daydream, hoping that the miracle will happen one day.

My own approach to this problem was, when I desperately wanted a large painting by a famous artist to go on an empty wall and knowing full well that I did not have the couple of million needed to buy it nor the twenty thousand a year to insure it, rather than leave the wall empty I would make do with a good copy. If and when I could afford the real thing, then I would replace the copy with the original. The funny thing was that when the time came, I could not bear to part with my nice copy.

The all-time classic example of reproductions becoming fakes concerned some Japanese copies of tower pistols. They were not bad but not copies of any particular model. No attempt had been made even to drill a touch-hole and overall they were jolly good furnishing pieces, made to sell at about £12. A genuine tower pistol at that time would have sold for £80 or £90. They were bright and shiny, so we were asked could we make them more authentic looking by adding a few marks and dulling them down a bit. With a set of punches, we added funny markings such as QE2, IRA, and PBI plus some anagrams of rather rude words. They were then suspended in the gents' toilet for a few days and came out duller than they went in, for which we charged an extra couple of quid. The end result was ideal for what it was meant for – i.e., decorating, and priced accordingly with 'reproduction pistols' written on the price tag. In the opinion of all who saw them, they could not in a month of Sundays be mistaken for original pistols.

The first sign that we might be mistaken was when a very senior police officer phoned me and asked if I knew of any major theft from a museum or arsenal of flintlock pistols. I wondered at the time why he assumed that if a theft had occurred that I would know about it. He then explained that his men had seen a well-known group of fringe dealers and villains with a plentiful supply of tower pistols which he was sure they had not come by legally. He went on to explain that despite making extensive enquiries of the various museums and military establishments, none had apparently lost anything. I too made enquiries but also drew a blank. A detective inspector was dispatched to me with one of the offending pistols which they had managed to acquire, and as soon as I saw it I realised what had happened. The inspector was taken to the storeroom and shown the remaining boxful and invited to the gents' to view the ageing process. I dread to think how many police hours were expended on operation 'Flintlock'.

Dear old Jimmy Goode came to see me one day and asked, 'You got rid of those damn Japanese pistols?' I told him no, I still had a few left and asked did he want some. 'Not bloody likely, I bought a pair of the buggers down in the West Country and paid £100 for them thinking they were right.' I did not press the matter but guessed what had happened. Jimmy, smashing bloke though he was, would play these silly games of feigning disinterest in any item that he really wanted in the hope of getting it cheap. In all probability the guns were in a dark corner of a shop and the dealer was asking £120. Jimmy, knowing that a matched brace of tower pistols were worth at that time over £200, put on his disinterested act and rather than ask to look closely at the pistols grudgingly offered £100. It was only later when he inspected his 'bargain' properly that he realised that he had stuffed himself up. Being the big man he was, he ruefully accepted that it was all part of the game and did not go back crying and stamping his feet as so many so-called dealers would today.

The final twist in the saga of these pistols came when a nice old gent was looking around the shop and spotted them. He bought a pair for £25. Some weeks later, the same old gent returned and bought another pair. After several more pairs, I asked him what he was doing with them and he explained: 'It's all rather odd, Mr Rothery. For many years, I had a pair of genuine pistols hung in my hall. One day, one of these chaps who goes round knocking on doors to buy antiques called and offered me £50 for them, which I took. I regretted it after because the wall looked bare without them so, when I saw those reproductions of yours, I bought them and put them up in the vacant space. A few weeks later, another guy came along and he offered me £100 for the ones I got from you. Knowing I could get more from you, I let him have them and it has gone on from there.'

I asked him what area he lived in and when he told me I immediately realised that it was right on the route that the Brighton knocker boys operated along. This is indeed a bit of a reversal on the usual stories we hear.

What happened to all the pistols in the end I have no idea, but I would not mind betting that they have passed through many hands over the years and are still adorning the wall of some proud owner.

Here I am, writing about not trying to be clever and sticking to the subject and warning you to be careful about buying things in the dark backs of shops. At the same time, I am having a little smile because sitting on my desk next to the word processor is a bronze. The story of how it came to be there might amuse you.

One morning as I was hurrying to my shop, I was accosted by a dealer who in a very conspiratorial manner took me to the dimly-lit back of his establishment where he produced a cloth-wrapped package from a drawer.

'Look, Mr Rothery, I bought this chest and when I got it home I found this in one of the drawers. I want to get shot of it before the wife sees it. Is it worth £25 to you?' My first thought was that the object was a gun of some sort, so I was somewhat surprised when he unwrapped the package to see a bronze of two young ladies who were obviously very fond of each other. Now, while bronzes are not my field, I do know a little about them, including the fact that erotic bronzes made in France, as this one was, fetched ten times what the guy was asking. The weight was right, the baize cloth on the base was worn with a few moth holes and it had the right sort of ageing with a lovely patina.

At the first opportunity, I phoned a friend of mine who I knew had a client for this sort of thing. I gave him an accurate description of measurements, weight, subject and signature. 'Oh yes, I know about those. The boys in Brighton are having them made in the Far East and knocking them out to the trade at £7 each.'

For some time I had it on my desk at the shop, where unfortunately (much to the annoyance of their partners) it evoked an unhealthy interest from some of the lady clients. It was then brought home and now sits on my desk as a constant reminder to me to follow my own advice.

Composite items

'What on earth are they?' you ask, so I'll tell you. A composite item is a 'bitsa': something made up of bitsa this and bitsa that from numerous different articles and periods and cobbled together at some time or another for purely utility purposes. You, my friend, are going to meet many such articles in your collecting career. Do not be frightened of them, they are a great source of fun and a fascinating, if sometimes frustrating, subject in their own right.

Most common are the big pieces of furniture which have been cut down to fit into a smaller house or the D-end table made up with a top from the side of a Georgian wardrobe and legs from a Victorian four-poster bed. You will find the set of chairs, six made in 1795, and an additional four in 1820 when the owner bought a bigger house, almost a perfect match but different dates and probably different makers.

On a grander scale, Lord Muckpiddle has place settings for 50 people made at a fashionable porcelain factory in 1795. Ten years later, he buys a bigger house and has the same factory make another 50 settings to the same design. Twenty years after that, his son replaces all the bits that the staff have broken and so it goes on for a couple of centuries. What do we have today? An almost complete dinner service for 100 people with several different years of manufacture, but all identical.

The military were always modifying their guns and swords. Indeed, there is one model of 'Brown Bess' which was made up of all the odds and ends of spares lying in the various arsenals. You would be hard put to find two identical, but it was an official model. Which reminds me of an occasion when a collector commented, 'I think the cock on that musket is a replacement.' To which the dealer replied, 'After two hundred years yours might be.'

In addition to all these mysteries, there are the things that have been repaired or restored possibly more than once over the years, with varying degrees of skill and accuracy. How then do we view this hotchpotch of dates, styles and materials?

Some people would dismiss the reproductions, copies and composite items as not worth bothering with and we do have such snobs in the collecting fraternity. But I would suggest that if for reasons of finance or security or just for the hell of it you fancy collecting them, then why on earth not?

Fakes

To me, this describes an object which has been deliberately manufactured or altered so as to mislead or fool. Not, I may add, always for financial gain. It will no doubt surprise you that, in all my years in the trade, I have rarely come across this.

Many talented people who cannot afford rare items have taken it upon themselves to make those items in an attempt to emulate the skills of their predecessors. Others who are missing a rare version of whatever they collect will get a common model and modify it to look like the rare one for no other reason than to fill the gap in their collection and with no intention of selling it for profit.

It is only when these items drift into the public domain and get into the hands of the fly types that they start getting passed off as originals at inflated prices and the trouble starts. The situation is rather akin to what I said about reproductions.

'What about provenance?' you ask. Well, you do not really think that villains with the knowledge and skill to fake great works of art are not going to employ those same skills to fake a perfectly plausible provenance do you? You will see an example of this in a story I shall tell later. The other problem with very old items is: how far back does the provenance go?

Recently I turned down a twelfth-century sword with an impeccable pedigree showing it to have been in a certain castle since the fifteenth century. But where was it, if it even existed, for the missing 300 years? This is a problem which creates endless argument among academics regarding many of the paintings in our national galleries.

We lesser mortals really do not need to worry about such matters since the things we collect are not of sufficient value to attract the professional faker. He or she is not going to waste their time producing things which are only going to sell for a few hundred pounds or less.

Here are a few examples of what really happens in real life, rather than in the fertile imaginations of the 'experts'.

Let us take the case of a wonderful artist, Mr Keating, who a few years back was taken before the courts and convicted on a charge of forgery. This gentleman was a very talented artist with an in-depth knowledge of the history of art who, for his own amusement, painted pictures in the style of various famous painters, reproducing their brushwork and colours with great accuracy. He was also very gifted in various methods of ageing these pictures. He was, in all probability, thoroughly fed up with the posing and prattling of the 'arty-farty brigade' who, when he showed them the pictures, banged on about 'unknown works' and 'contemporary copies'. He then took great delight in telling them they were talking through their hats, as he had painted them last week.

He became something of a local celebrity and earned a small living by his copies, which, incidentally, he never signed in the original artist's name and only occasionally in his own. He also charged very little for his work so he was in no way a professional faker intent on cheating anybody. Unfortunately, his works did get into the hands of less scrupulous persons who did add the original artists' signatures and sold the results to gullible people as genuine. Hence the court case and his subsequent conviction.

It was probably instigated by either a member of the art establishment who had had their nose put out of joint by being fooled by one of Mr Keating's works, or one of those pathetic little twerps who cries blue murder when he finds that he has not got the better of a deal. Mr Keating did, towards the end of his life, enjoy some recognition and appeared in a TV series about art, which was, in my opinion, one of those extremely rare TV programmes with any degree of integrity.

What then do we call this gentleman's work? Personally, I would call him a *copyist*. The people who added the signatures were the fakers. Regretfully, I do not have an example of his work but I would be proud to have one in my home. Mr Keating was my sort of bloke. He looked the 'experts' in the eye, then spat in it!

The only major faking that I have personal experience of concerned a number of pistols. The story, I think, is well worth telling because, while I have chosen to include it in this chapter, it illustrates many other facets of the collecting scene.

Hughie Nimmo was a genius. He had served his apprenticeship as a toolmaker and then served during the war as a chief engine room artificer in the Royal Navy, mostly on submarines and earning a well deserved Distinguished Service Medal. Notwithstanding that he appeared to live entirely on a diet of Earl Grey tea and malt whisky (mostly the latter), he could do almost anything with wood or metal. He was also a very keen and knowledgeable collector, which is how I came to meet him.

Hughie often did small repair jobs for me and one day I was showing him the remains of a seventeenth-century pistol which, in its time, had been a superb specimen but was now, even though most of the major parts were there, little more than a relic.

Jokingly, I commented, 'I think that's beyond even your talents, Hughie.'

He looked at me over the top of his half-moon glasses. 'Aye,' he replied, 'it wud be a bloody sight easier to make a new one.' No more was said and later he went off home, taking the gun with him 'to look at'.

Some weeks later, I was just locking up the shop when the phone went. It was, of course, the good Hughie. 'Wid ye be coming round for a cup of Earl Grey, John?'

Ten minutes later I was at the house.

What our hero had done was to read everything he could

find on this type of gun, but more importantly the methods of manufacture and tools used in the 1600s. His conclusion was that, if we were thinking of making one of these pistols, the only proper thing to do would be to make the tools in use at that time and then learn to use them. This called for hand-twisting and hammering the barrel on a mandrill, then making a rifling machine from leather and bones. Also the screws would have to be cast and then hand-threaded. I agreed to fund all the research and raw materials on the condition that if it worked we would go into production with an eye to the black powder shooting market.

Months went by and the problems we came across were many and complex. For instance, the correct formula to make the fluid for colouring the barrel called for fresh oak chips and cow urine. The problem of getting the right wood for the stock was resolved by purchasing the whole root of a cherry tree from a pipe manufacturer. For months Hughie practised using the tools as well as learning and practising the art of metal engraving.

I had almost forgotten that the experiment was going on when one day Hughie called and asked, 'What name were you thinking of putting on the pistol?' After much thought, we decided that the best maker of the time was a chap called Tarles, so it had better be him.

More months went by, when again the phone went. 'Wid ye be coming round for a cup of Earl Grey, John?' Minutes later I was at his house. With great pride, he pushed away the near-empty Glenfiddich bottle and lovingly unwrapped the finished article. I am not often lost for words but I was speechless as I saw there, gently gleaming at me, the most perfect example of a 1660s Tarles pistol, complete with the rather ornate lock plate which he had reproduced perfectly. Or had he? Warning bells sounded in my mind, and then I spotted what was wrong.

'Hughie, you daft bastard. Tarles is spelt Tarles, not

114

Tarleys.' Somehow (maybe the near empty bottle was a clue) the dear man had got muddled with the ornate engraving and mistaken a piece of trailing vine for a Y. We were now the proud possessors of a perfect specimen of a seventeenth-century flintlock pistol with a rifled screw barrel, but unfortunately apparently the work of a non-existent gunmaker.

Hughie, bless him, was not put out in the slightest. When I had calmed down, he explained to me that he had taken the opportunity when making each component part of making several spares at the same time, so it was now no problem with his newly acquired skills and the spare parts to make another. In fact, it had always been his opinion that we should have made a pair in the first place, which is what he now intended to do.

The misspelt Tarleys was consigned to a drawer and a few weeks later a pair of superb Tarles was delivered.

Hughie asked me if I wanted any more because, while he had plenty of spare parts he had got the taste for pistol-making and rather fancied having a go at making other types. This he did and produced, among other things, a fine pair of Voges pistols with multi-groove rifling, and several tower long sea service pistols.

With the financial side of the experiment having proved to be a complete disaster and not wishing to commit myself to yet more extremely expensive pistols, I was quite happy for Hughie to go off and enjoy his own experiments.

For months, I had tremendous sport with my Tarles, using them alternatively as a sort of test piece on some of the self proclaimed 'experts' who saw them and, I am ashamed to admit, revelling in their discomfort when they invariably mis-read them. I also used them as a sort of visual training aid when trying to educate the more worthwhile collectors.

Eventually, there occurred what I can only call a visitation from a representative of a well-known auction house. While in my shop, he espied the Tarles and, before I could say a word, the idiot committed what I consider to be a cardinal sin. He launched into a long-winded lecture about them – date, type, maker and method of operating. Hardly the sort of thing that hard-nosed professional dealers with donkeys' years of experience want to hear from self-opinionated little farts who were not even born when that dealer started their career.

He then condescendingly informed me that his company would be happy to enter them in their next sale and could he please take them with him to display at a forthcoming arms fair. Stifling the urge to tell him that I was quite capable of selling my stock without the aid of his auction house and relishing the thought of the almighty bollocking he was going to get when the real experts at head office saw them, I agreed.

'Well, young sir,' said I, in my most deferential manner, 'if you think they are worthy of your attention, by all means take them with you but may I have a receipt please?'

'Quite right,' he said, talking down to me in the manner that all auction house employees adopt when addressing the very people that provide their living. 'You should always ask for a receipt, even from us.'

He duly signed the paper on which I had written 'One pair of flintlock pistols', with no mention of date or any further description, and off he went happy as a sandboy.

I waited with ill-contained amusement for the reaction when he showed the pistols to his masters. Nothing. I then waited for a greater reaction when they appeared at the arms fair. Nothing.

Eventually, young Rupert phoned me and to my utter amazement informed me that there had been a lot of interest at the fair and he intended to put them into the next connoisseur's sale. Did I want to give them a description or would I leave it to them? And what about a reserve?

No, said I, I'll leave all that to you. I did ask him if there had been any adverse comment about the pistols at the fair. 'Oh no,' he said 'there was one old boy who said he thought

116

they might have been re-stocked and they looked too good to be true, but we didn't take any notice of the old chap.'

I found out later that the 'old chap' to whom he was referring was none other than Mr Marcus Dineley, one of the shrewdest and most knowledgeable men that ever walked this earth.

The Tarles did appear in the sale and made a near record price. I kept very quiet.

The next stage of this ongoing saga started when, many months later, young Rupert wafted into the shop, still very much full of his own wind and importance, and greeted me with, 'Hello, Mr Rothery, just passing.' Oscar Wilde came to mind and the occasion when a friend informed him that he had passed his house the previous evening, to which Oscar replied, 'Thank you, dear boy, thank you.'

Rupert then informed me that, in the unlikely event of a back street junk shop like mine getting any more fine pistols, he might be willing to appraise them for me. I blush to admit I lost my rag. 'Look, you supercilious little sod! Are you cognizant of the fact that the last pair were fakes?'

From the position of safety that he had taken up behind a rather large cannon, he quavered. 'Oh no, Mr Rothery, I think we should have known if that were the case.'

'Too bloody right you "should" have known, but you didn't!' I roared at him. 'Now how do you feel about another pair exactly the same and what name would you like on them?'

Feeling reassured by the arrival of my manager, the late Alan Jaimeson, who had positioned his 18 stone between the two of us, Rupert reappeared from behind the cannon and rather nervously informed me, 'Mr Rothery, I feel sure you are joking, but should another pair of pistols like the last ones come up we would want some sort of provenance on them.'

He then departed, probably with considerable relief that he had survived the encounter physically unscathed.

As soon as he was out of the building I was on the phone to Hughie.

'How soon can you do me another pair of those screw-barrel pistols?'

'Aboot six weeks.'

'Right, get started...' A pause. '...And Hughie, stay off the malt until they are finished.'

Another pause. 'Wid ye be wanting the same name on them?'

Even longer pause. 'I'll let you know.'

Portsmouth is a city that I love dearly despite what Hitler did to it during the Second World War and what successive councils have done to it since. For years, I have taken a deep interest in the old girl's history which is how I know that, during the time that Samuel Pepys was secretary to the Navy in the seventeenth century, whenever his duties brought him to Portsmouth he always took lodgings with a family in the High Street, Old Portsmouth. Sam was a bit of a ladies' man and it is alleged that he had a warm relationship with the lady of the house. It is also alleged that one night, when the lady's husband came home unexpectedly, Sam was obliged to make a hasty exit, in the process of which he inadvertently left his pistols behind. The man of the house, finding them one day in his wife's wardrobe, not unreasonably sought an explanation from her as to what the pistols were doing there. She, with the cunning that is inherent in all of the fairer sex, burst into tears and told him that they were meant to be a surprise present from Sam on the husband's forthcoming birthday but now he had spoilt the surprise. Sam, of course, had no choice but to back the good lady's story – it was a time, remember, when duelling was prevalent.

For many generations the family told the story of Sam's pistols whenever they were brought out to be shown to visitors. During the Second World War, that area was extensively bombed and, as with so many things, the pistols were lost.

Samuel Pepys' gunmaker was a chap called Truelock. Guess what the name on the next pair of pistols was going to be!

'Sleazies,' drawled the voice.

'Good morning. My name is Rothery. May I please speak to Mr Rupert Golightly-Smith?'

'Does he know you?' asked the voice.

'Not, fortunately, in the biblical sense, but I have put some items through your sales and he did ask me to contact him if any more came along.'

'I will ask if he will speak to you.' That's big of you, I thought.

Eventually, the wee man came on the line and I informed him that I had another pair of pistols exactly like the last ones but this time by Truelock.

'You mean in the same style?'

'No. I mean exactly the same.'

'I shall be in Portsmouth in a couple of weeks and shall try to find time to come in and have a look at them.'

Sure enough, a couple of weeks later, in he came. A little less bumptious and full of himself, so I thought, maybe he is learning. But oh no. He fiddled about with the pistols for a time, and then his ego took over again.

'Well, they are not exactly the same, but you can be for-given for thinking so since they are very much in the style of the others but a few years later I would say. It is a little worry-ing that two such similar pairs of pistols should appear in such a short time and bearing in mind your jocular remarks last time we met. Do you have any provenance on them?'

I told him that they were supposedly once the property of Samuel Pepys and that he had given them to the family he stayed with in Portsmouth when he was secretary to the Navy, but that personally I didn't believe a word of it.

Off he went with the pistols to get them 'looked at'.

I suppose several weeks had gone by when I was again called to the phone. 'Hello, Mr Rothery. Golightly-Smith here, and I've got some very good news for you. Those pistols are as right as ninepence and our researchers have confirmed that Truelock was Pepys' gunmaker. Furthermore, he did give them to the family that he stayed with in Portsmouth; there are several references to this in his diaries!'

I thought, thank God I never buy anything off this lot.

The pistols did not sell in the next auction having failed to reach reserve; maybe people were waking up. In only a matter of days I was called yet again to the phone. 'My name is Snodgrass. I was the under bidder for the Truelocks and I understand you are the vendor.'

Guilt put me immediately on my guard. 'Yes, sir.'

'Well, I am wondering if you can tell me anything about them as I bought an almost identical pair in a previous auction but by Tarles.'

Oh deary me, I thought. It's money-back time.

'Not very much, I'm afraid, but if you are at all unhappy...'

Before I could say more, he cut in with, 'My dear chap, it's nothing like that. I've been collecting this type of pistol for years. As a matter of fact, I'm writing a book about them. No. I'm interested in buying the pistols and since I did not get them in the sale, I wondered what you would take for them?'

'Look, sir, are you really sure about these pistols?'

Without a moment's hesitation, he launched into a long lecture about what an expert he was and stopped just short of what a cretin I was.

'Ok sir. Send me a cheque for so much and I'll tell the auction people to let you have the guns. But I am not banking your cheque until I hear from you that you are completely satisfied with them.'

In what seemed like no time, he was back onto me to tell me that he had compared the two sets of pistols and, in his opinion, not only had the same man made them all, but the wood had come from the same tree on all of them. He then explained that the actual maker was probably a Dutch outworker who made guns for both Tarles and Truelock about 1663. No argument from me could persuade him otherwise and I was to bank his cheque forthwith.

He did write his book, God bless him, and I think one of Hughie's works of art was illustrated with a description and dated about 1663. I would have put the date as 1973!

If anyone knows where those pistols are today, I would love to buy them back.

Things started to go a bit wrong for poor old Hughie and he hit a rather bad patch so, in an effort to help him, I bought his other pistols including the Voges and some of the sea service pistols, the intention being that when he recovered he could buy them back. It might have been the whisky, I doubt if it was the Earl Grey, but dear Hughie never recovered and went to join the great gunmaker in the sky.

At one time, I used to make a trip down to Cornwall about every six weeks. These trips always included a visit to a wonderful character by the name of Bertie Curnow, who was not only a very shrewd and experienced dealer but a good friend to me in my early days. Bertie had one particular quirk which was, if you told him that something was not for sale he had to try to buy it. One night, I was having a sandwhich with him and his wife before setting off back to Hampshire and, on opening my briefcase, Bertie spotted the Voges which, for some reason or another, I had with me.

'Wot eee got there then? You English is allus coming down from upalong an robbing us poor Cornishmen. Come on, lets 'ave a look at 'em.'

'Bertie, you really would not want them and they are not for sale anyway.'

That, of course, was a challenge to him. He went on and on until I agreed to let him buy them for £600. He immediately gave me the money, but I left it on the table when the time came to go and told him, 'Bertie, those pistols are fakes. Take your money back.'

He sat back in some amazement and only finally believed me when I removed one of the locks and showed him Hughie's deliberate mistake. Then, pushing the money towards me, he said, 'These have got to be the finest set of pistols made this century. I wouldn't let you have them back at twice the money.'

I left Bertie that night a far happier man than if I had sold him an original pair of pistols.

When, as I told you, Hughie died, his widow let me have some of his early work, including the sea service and the mis-spelt Tarleys. What happened to the sea service I can't remem-

'Of course I want it today. If I had wanted it tomorrow, I would have brought it in tomorrow!'

ber, but I do recall he always marked the woodwork 05 and the originals were invariably marked 06. Hughie, being an old Royal Navy man, always said that was because 05 was the Battle of Trafalgar. The Tarleys I sold to dear old Ray Coker because he would not accept that it was not right and when I called his bluff to my horror he put his money down. I deeply regret selling it, not for Ray's sake, he got what he deserved, but that pistol was my last link with a great man and a dear friend.

Mr Keating's paintings are, I am told, much sought after by people who collect his and other artists fakes. Bertie was over the moon with his fake Voges pistols and had great fun with them. I am desperate to buy back Hughie's pistols out of sheer sentiment and equally keen to buy one of Mr Keating's pictures.

From all this, one might then draw the conclusion that if it's a good fake with a good story, then surely it can only add to your collection, not detract from it, by being there.

8

Restoration and Repairs

Here, I must admit to being at something of a loss as to what to advise. On the one hand, I am always telling people that, by definition, most antiques have had a long life and much use so we must expect and accept the odd bit of damage here and there and live with it. Also, I tell them that antiques should glow but never shine.

My own view is that I would much rather have a piece with honourable wounds rather than an obvious repair. Personally, I would not countenance anything in my house that has been 'over-restored'. The obvious example of this is the vintage car with the undercoat showing through the original paint rather than the same vehicle with an obvious recent respray. It is rather like being seen out with a lady 'of a certain age' who has matured gracefully as opposed to some poor old soul with too many face-lifts. Beauty is indeed in the eye of the beholder because on the other hand I tell people to do in their house, with their collection, whatever they like best and not to give a jot for what 'they say'.

Buying things to have 'done up' by professional restorers is rather a mixed blessing. Chairs and sofas are no great problem as there is a multitude of good upholsterers and you get the coverings of your choice. The same can be said of most furniture. The fairly large numbers of restorers creates a degree of competition, which in turn keeps the cost down.

This also applies to silver and jewellery and the other more common collectables. The problems start when you collect the less fashionable items. Who, for instance, do we know who can restore old optical instruments or antique embroidery, let alone old ship models, rocking horses or early aeroplanes? There are such people but the problem is finding them and getting our treasures to them.

As always I am talking about professional people and not the sub-species of trade groupies who do these things in their spare time and invariably with no proper training. If you trust your valuables to them and they cock it up, there would be little point in going to court and getting several thousand pounds compensation from someone who lives in a council house, has five kids and a car on HP and will never be in a position to pay any amount that the court awards.

The next consideration is the cost factor. Highly skilled and talented restorers expect, quite rightly, to be paid for their skills and they don't come cheap, especially if they are in one of those areas where there are not many of them and hence not much competition.

We are back to the question of philosophy. Is your aim to get some rare and beautiful artefact returned to all its former glory regardless of cost? If so, we do not have a great problem. Nothing is impossible given limitless time and a blank cheque. Is your thought that having an old, damaged item restored is cheaper than buying a good specimen or that the item will be worth more when it is restored? Maybe, but unlikely. True, it can happen with a little bit of luck but not as a general rule. It usually works out like this.

The collector sees a Nagasaki bus stop, which is normally in a shop for £200 being offered at £50. They buy it and to get a proper job done pay say £100. Add the cost of transport and the final figure comes out at about £180, so they have saved £20. Hell of a lot of effort and messing about for £20, don't you think? Of course, if they want to sell it, they will be lucky to get their money back.

This sort of arithmetic applies equally to the trade. Very often we will have an item marked at £100 which done up would fetch £200. The cost of the work plus, in our case, the item being out of stock while it is done, outweighs whatever little extra we would get for it, so we sell it for £100.

The reverse of this is true if you have an item worth £20,000 restored that you can buy for £10,000 and then spend £5,000 having it worked on by a top restorer. Even if you wait six months for it, the operation becomes worthwhile.

My own personal error of judgement is still in my lounge. While buying a cannon from a chap, I saw an interesting looking chest in the same barn. I enquired as to what it was and was informed that it was a 'table-top piano', dated 1771 and made by Kirkman, who was the top maker of the time. The owner explained that he had had it appraised and that fully restored it was worth thousands, but to do this would cost the best part of £2,000. He then told me that, as he did not have the money to pay for the restoration and was moving house the next day; I could have it for £100. Knowing full well that I was going to make more than that out of the cannon, I agreed.

Having sorted out the cannon, I then phoned a pal of mine who was a director of one of the 'Super Sleazies' and asked if they had such a thing as an antique piano expert. He put me onto a nice young lady who listened to my story and then went on and on enthusing over my discovery of the Kirkman. She confirmed all the vendor had told me and recommended the only man in the country who could be trusted with the sacred task of restoration. The great man agreed to see me and it was arranged that I should take the thing to him on, of all days, Boxing Day.

Having examined the piano, he went into raptures about it and said he would be honoured to save such an important piece for posterity. While he was not prepared to commit to a completion date, he did estimate that it would cost about

£2,000 and he would like a deposit of £500. Some six months later, he contacted me and explained that he had a problem. The hammer springs were made of ivory and with the new laws on the sale of ivory, he was having trouble getting a supply. Could I, with my contacts in the antique trade, get hold of any Victorian corsets? The bones in them were made of ivory and ideal for what he wanted. I got some very funny looks when I started asking my friends in the trade for Victorian corsets, but get them I did and they were delivered to my restorer.

Just before the following Christmas, he called me and told me the job was finished but I could not collect it yet because he wanted to enjoy playing it and he felt that as it was delivered on Boxing Day it would be nice if it was collected on Boxing Day ... and, by the way, I owed him £1,500 balance on the job. No two ways about it, he had done a first class job and it was with considerable pride that I installed it in the lounge.

Unfortunately, we do not have any pianists in my family and after a while I felt guilty about it lying idle, when someone who could play it might appreciate it more. Once again, I contacted the lady antique piano expert who again went into raptures about it and arranged to drop in and see it when she was visiting friends in the area. When she came, she sat and played it and said her company would be delighted to have it in one of its specialist sales. I broached the question of money, to hear, 'Oh, Mr Rothery, it should do very well and could fetch as much as £800 or £900!'

As I said, it now lives in the lounge and I reckon I have had my money's worth, if only from the enjoyment my guests get from me telling the story.

'What about if I buy it and restore it myself?' I have no wish to be rude but I have seen more antiques ruined by amateur restorers than you would believe. Perhaps. If you served a seven-year apprenticeship as a restorer.

I do beg your pardon but there are many who attempt restoration whose enthusiasm is far greater than their talents. So assuming that you are not a professional but fancy having a go then why not indeed, providing we approach the subject with caution.

You could consider a full-time course at one of the top schools, such as West Dean College in Sussex, whose curriculum covers a whole range of restoration skills. If you do not have the time, the money or the inclination to do that, then most local education authorities run evening classes, which might well include something to suit you. While I do strongly recommend some sort of formal training, if you already have artistic or manual skills then at least buy a few books on your subject.

Whatever avenue of learning you select, please do not try to run before you can walk. Practise and experiment on rubbish, which, if you cock it up, is no great loss to you or posterity. Only when you are confident in your skills should you start on the good stuff. 'Common sense', I hear you cry again. Yes, I know it is, but you would be amazed at how often I see nice things ruined by inexperienced restorers, such as the guy recently who took £3,000 off the price of a pair of pistols by trying to clean them!

'You should never clean things' is another of those bits of advice we often hear, and in the main it is true. But you will not do a lot of harm if you remove the top layer of cobwebs and dust with a feather duster or soft cloth. It is only when people try to polish things with abrasives that it gets dangerous. The best course of action before attempting anything is to take it to your tame local dealer and seek advice; yet another reason for building up that relationship that I keep telling you about.

Assuming you attain a degree of skill, then you are in the enviable position of being able to buy the tired items at lower prices and, assuming you don't mind the time taken, restore them to your liking, thus improving the quality of your collection at little or no cost.

When considering a restoration, borrow my family motto: 'Festina lente', which, roughly translated, means 'proceed with caution'.

9

Security and Insurance

'I'm looking for antiques.'

This is a subject to which collectors as a rule give little, if any, thought. Common sense should tell us that in this day and age, with the crime rate constantly rising, it is advisable to do all we can to protect our homes and loved ones. Add the temptation of even the most modest collection and our homes become yet more of a target.

This is, of course, no reason why we should not collect but we must take basic precautions to lessen the risk to our children, our homes and our collection – in that order.

Let us first consider the house. Are you sure that the locks on the windows and doors are of sufficient quality to stop any attempts at break-ins? Or are they the ones that were there when you moved in? Why not take advice from your local police station where there is a crime prevention officer who will be only too happy to advise you, or talk to the person in the security shop. It may well cost you money to update your security but it will cost you a damn sight more if you lose your collection, let alone how you will live with yourself if the wife or kids get hurt.

We now come to the question of what I call 'personal security'. It is not much use if, having turned your house in to a mini Fort Knox, the wife nips out to the corner shop and leaves the front door open. 'Common sense', you cry, so why do so many people do it?

One thing that many collectors do not do is to give some thought to the positioning and display of their collection. Your postman and milkman are decent people doing a worthwhile job in all weathers. They are as honest as the day is long but they are human. Back at the depot or in the pub after work, it is not uncommon for them to say to their mates, 'I was doing a delivery today to that house on the corner of Accacia Avenue. You should have seen the lovely stuff they have; the bloke there is a bit of a collector.'

Of course, your tradespeople are not going to creep back in the middle of the night and rob you, but what about the guy further down the bar nursing a half pint and listening to everything?

One collector I knew got burgled with monotonous regularity. He lived in a first floor apartment outside of which was a bus stop. Hence, every 20 minutes the passengers on the upper deck of the bus got a grandstand view of his collection, and not all those passengers were nice people. It never occurred to the fool to put his collection where it could not be seen from the road or even to pull his curtains.

Another collector living in a terraced house fronting onto the pavement actually put items in his window. He hoped I think that somebody might see them and offer him something else for his collection. Well, somebody most certainly did see them and admire them, with the result that they took them one night without bothering to open the window. He lost not only his goodies, but the price of a new window. You might say he was too clever for his own good.

Here, I have to confess that I too nearly did something equally stupid. I lived at the time in a very nice apartment in a block overlooking the Canoe Lake and public gardens in Southsea, with a wonderful view of the Solent. The main feature of the lounge was a superb chimney-breast, which cried out for a really nice piece to set it off to its full advantage. After much searching and at a price which frightened the bank manager, I found the ideal thing in the form of an oil painting of some importance.

With great care, this was mounted on my chimney-breast and I was over the moon with the result. That night, when I took the dog out for a walk, I glanced up at my apartment and there it was! My lovely painting lit up like a display in a high street window, an open invitation to every footpad and villain that passed by.

Well, what could I do? If I kept the curtains drawn, I blotted out the view of the Solent. If I left the curtains open, I was likely to have a break-in and not only lose the picture but suffer untold damage to the apartment and possibly myself. The picture was moved.

Having spent many years and much money in assembling a collection, some people then seem to hold a sort of deathwish with regards to its safety. They are, of course, inordinately proud of their collection and, with some reason, wish to show it off to others. That is perfectly understandable, but the willingness with which they invite complete strangers into their homes exceeds any normal standards of hospitality and questions their mental soundness.

An example of this was when a complete stranger who was visiting Portsmouth informed me that the previous evening he had met the secretary of the local rifle and pistol club in a pub. He had invited the stranger back to his house and shown him all the club's firearms and thrown in a lecture on how to use them for good measure. I did not let on to the stranger that I knew the gentleman concerned, but gently questioned him and, within half an hour, he had divulged to me the secretary's name and address and what pub he used. I wondered what untold damage might have occurred if that information had got into the wrong hands. I put it all down to yet another example of enthusiasm getting the better of common sense.

The ghastly TFI shot himself in the foot yet again on this question of personal security, or in his case lack of it, when the devious, greedy sod had the brilliant idea of waylaying the knockers when they returned from their raids. He would skulk outside the various shops and approach them with the exhortation that they should deal with him direct, to which end he gave them his home address and phone number. It worked. They all went round to his house and he showed them his collection. It was only after he had been robbed for the umpteenth time and could no longer get insurance cover at any price that it dawned on him that perhaps it wasn't such a good idea after all.

There was an interesting spin-off to this little saga.

Most dealers, regardless of what you see on TV, will not

knowingly touch stolen goods with a bargepole. They are extremely fuzz-friendly and willingly cooperate with the police when it comes to catching thieves and recovering stolen goods. The officer in charge of TFI's case asked me why, on this occasion, the dealers were not showing their usual willingness to help. When I explained the circumstances to him, he thought for a moment and said, 'Well, the bastard deserved all he got. I think we've wasted too much time on this case anyway.'

If you are ever approached by a local newspaper or TV station with a request to feature you and your collection, be *very* careful. You may be rather pleased with this recognition and you might be tempted to think that the article or feature could lead to you meeting other collectors, being offered nice things and that your appearance will give you credibility with the local dealers. What is more likely is that, despite assurances from the media, they will probably misquote you and mention the road and area where you live, with the result that it will not take a genius to work out your exact address should a villain wish to visit you. Probably, some idiot will read the article or watch the programme and immediately claim that the item you were showing was stolen from them years ago. I assure you this is true. I once showed an item on TV, which, within 24 hours was claimed by three different people, all swearing that it was pinched from them at different times and from different parts of the country.

Far from your credibility improving, the local dealers will think you're a plonker for getting sucked into giving the interview in the first place. Once again, I beg you to think hard before letting strangers, least of all the media, anywhere near your collection.

I am not for one minute suggesting that you go home and sit in a locked and darkened room slavering over your collection like a demented Silas Marley. Only that you take the trouble and show sense enough to be careful.

One final point I would mention is the rather odd people

who buy things and then put them in a bank vault. These strange creatures profess to be collectors but it is beyond me how anyone can call themselves a collector when they immediately consign beautiful and desirable artefacts to a hole in the ground where no one can see and enjoy them. It seems to make the whole idea of collecting completely pointless. Surely, if they were unable to ensure the safety of these things, it would make more sense for the owners to pass the items on to someone who is able to look after them properly and enjoy them at the same time. I think perhaps that the word 'hoarder' would better describe these people. I am sure it is a case of taking security to the extreme, if not the fringe of lunacy.

Having done all that is possible to ensure that our collection is as safe as we can make it, we must, of course, consider the question of insurance. Does anybody outside the insurance industry ever read a policy? The usual attitude is, 'Well, it's covered on the household insurance.'

Are you sure?

Many insurers specifically exclude collections. Nearly all insist that special arrangements have to be made for items over a certain value. On your policy, would a collection be considered a single item or would each individual piece be defined as a single item? I don't know. Do you? Because if you're not sure, you would be well advised to find out.

If you collect fragile or delicate things, such as porcelain, are you covered for accidents in the house? When you take your favourite piece to have it valued, cleaned or to show it at the club, is it covered while in transit?

These are all matters that you should give thought to and get cleared by your insurers.

About three times a week, I am contacted by either insurance assessors or people who have lost things, asking for a valuation on missing items. The descriptions are vague to say the least. 'It was a Nagasaki bus stop with red tassels on.' So what! Was it an original? Was it in good condition? What year

135

was it from? Only a dealer blessed with the gift of second sight or the latest state-of-the-art crystal ball can have even the vaguest idea as to an item's true value, unless they have seen and handled it.

When pressed, the dealer will probably make a wild guess. Usually, funnily enough, this seems to satisfy all concerned, but my fellow dealers and I always feel in these cases that either the claimant or the insurance company has got the rough end of the deal. TFI most certainly did when his insurers asked the local dealers for valuations.

'It is worth £100, but you should insure it for £150.' Why? I have always been confused by this strange approach to insurance valuations. In the case of the electric toaster, no problem. A new one today costs £50, so the replacement value of a second hand one is £25. The claimant who has lost a collection of gold sovereigns, which, in the 1970s, was valued at £120, each, can today replace them at £50 each, which is what the insurers will pay. Again, no problem. So the insurers pay out the 'replacement' value of each item, regardless of the amount for which it is insured.

When we come to antiques and collectables, it becomes a bit more difficult. The more common items are fairly readily available. For example, in my case, a Victorian Naval officer's sword in good condition has gone missing and a claim for £700 made on the insurance company. Their assessor contacts me and asks if I have an identical sword and, if so, how much does it cost? On being told yes and £300, the company then pays the claimant and tells them that they can get a replacement from Mr Rothery for that amount. The same procedures apply when the claims are for china, silver, etc.

It is in the case of the very rare and valuable object where the difficulties arise. If the missing object is as rare as rocking horse droppings and there are only two dealers in the country who could even hazard a guess as to its value, then it would make sense to value it at £100,000 and argue it out with the

136

insurance company, rather than insure it for £10,000, which of course the insurers will willingly pay without argument. But of course, this book is not aimed at the people who move in that rarefied atmosphere.

My feelings on the practice of winding on the value for insurance purposes are mixed. On the one hand, if you value the various items individually, then add up the total value and insure the house contents for that amount that would seem to make sense. Your premium will of course go up according to the value. You might also be bullied by the insurance company into fitting very expensive security and alarms. It is an endearing habit of many insurance companies that their demands for additional security are such that when it has all been fitted, the place is virtually burglar-proof and one is left wondering if, in that case, it needs insuring.

Another view of over-valuing is the possible suggestion that the average collector rarely has their collection revalued and the higher figure is to allow for inflation or increases in the price of antiques over the years. What happens, in that case, if inflation is low and antiques' prices fall?

There is yet another interpretation of the practice of over-valuing for insurance. Could it be the suggestion that insurance companies are fair game when it comes to making highly inflated claims? Take the case of the poor old widow of one of our war heroes, who had her husband's gallantry medal stolen. The whole thing was reported in our local rag with much comment on the lack of morality of the thieves and any dealers or collectors who would have bought such an item. There was an editorial on the subject of falling standards, even letters to the editor from 'disgusted of Southsea'.

The lady's 'friend' approached me and asked, in the circumstances, would I give a free valuation? Of course I did, and in writing. The type of medal concerned would have been priced at about £460 on the collectors' market.

Some weeks later, the 'friend' called on me and informed

me that the old girl's money had come through and would I please start looking for a medal for her. Naturally, I agreed, but being the nice guy I am, suggested that if she applied to the Royal Navy they might be able to supply a replacement from the medal office, which would have the added advantage of having our hero's number, rank and name on the rim, as did the original. She would, of course, have to pay for such a replacement.

Full of thanks, the 'friend' hurried off and, sure enough, the rag ran an article showing the old lady with the replacement medal as supplied by the Royal Navy. The 'friend' called in to see me and thank me for all my good advice. Again, in passing, I asked whether the Navy charged her for the medal and, if so, how much?

'Oh yes, Mr Rothery, but they were very good and even with VAT it only came to about £65.'

My next question caused the 'friend' to go a bright shade of purple and rapidly leave the shop. Having replaced the medal for £65, did the lady return the other £400 that the insurance company had paid out for a replacement? What price morals and honesty now?

That old girl and the benefit cheats at the fairs and boot sales are all guilty of what some people call victimless crime. But there are victims: you and I who have to pay extra taxes to keep the idle bums on benefit payments and have to face ever-increasing insurance premiums as a result of the fraudulently inflated claims by people who see cheating the insurance companies as the norm.

What then can we do should we have the misfortune to lose goods? Obviously, inform the police as soon as possible and supply them with a complete and accurate list of the missing items. It is, of course, a great help if you have had the foresight to photograph your collection and possibly mark each piece with the magic pencils that are available and show up under an ultraviolet light. You would be surprised at how often, given this accurate information, the police, with the help of the trade, not only get people's goods back, but apprehend a few criminals too. This can only be done with your help.

If, sadly, as a result of a fire, or for some other reason, you cannot get your goods back, then you will be in a strong position to speedily get an equitable settlement based on an accurate valuation of your treasures.

There is a point of law here. If you are paid out for any item that has gone missing, that item, in the event of it being recovered, is the property of the insurance company, not you. So, having made a claim, if you find the missing item in the attic or it is returned to you, it rests with you to inform the insurance company who will, in all probability, offer it back to you for whatever they paid out to you in the first place. Failure to inform them would make you liable to criminal charges carrying very severe penalties.

Here are a few tips that might help you.

When purchasing an item, ask for a receipt with a brief description. You will not get one at a boot sale or the lower end of the fairs, where they are unlikely to admit to making any sales in case it affects their unemployment benefit or housing allowance, let alone make the item traceable should the police be interested in it. Having met some of the so-called dealers at these events, it would not surprise me if they thought a receipt was something that told you how to make a jam sponge. Most certainly, the established shops and the dealers at the more reputable fairs will be more than happy to give you a proper receipt. Some establishments tend to put a description on the labels of their goods and, where this is the case, do be sure to keep the labels and put them somewhere safe unless, of course, there is a danger of the wrong person getting to see what you have been spending.

When you talk to the crime prevention people about your locks, take the opportunity to find out about marking your

'Damned antique dealer wanted to charge me just for a professional opinion"

collectables with the aforementioned magic pens which, as I understand it, will not damage your goods.

For some reason, which I have never understood, collectors will go to any lengths to avoid paying for a proper valuation of their collections. One solicitor actually asked, with great indignation, 'Mr Rothery, you surely don't expect me to pay just for your professional opinion.'

At the end of the day, and assuming your collection justifies it, the only safe and proper way is to get a dealer or valuer to do the job and provide you with the usual three copies: one for the insurance company, one to keep at the bank or other safe place and one to keep at home. It would rather defeat the object of this exercise were the one and only copy to be consumed by the same fire that has destroyed your collection.

While on the subject of valuations, let me warn you against a very unpleasant and dangerous practice in which some people indulge, usually to their cost and confusion. That is trying to get a free valuation by comparing something they have at home with a similar item on show in an antiques shop. For example, the brain picker asks, 'Could you tell me all about that item and the price?'

The dealer then politely describes the item and the price. The brain picker then announces, with a smug smile, that they have one exactly the same at home, sometimes adding, 'Only better.' That person has now, by their deviousness, completely queered their pitch with that dealer who, if they ever want any help or advice in the future, might well take the opportunity to even the score.

A scenario in my shop: 'Could you tell me all about that sword and what it's worth?'

'Certainly madam, but if when I have done so you tell me that you have one like it at home, only better, I might well use it on you.'

The honest way would be to explain that you have an item like the one over there and were wondering if the dealer would be kind enough to give you some information on it. What will then happen, in all probability, is the dealer will warn you of the dangers of their trying to give you information on something they have not seen and explain that, while you think yours is the same, it may have minor differences which could greatly affect the appraisal. The dealer may then invite you to bring your piece in so that they can appraise it properly. The end result being that you get accurate information and there is goodwill all round.

I suppose 90 per cent of the things that people claim to have at home which are supposedly exactly like the one in the shop turn out, on viewing, to be nothing like the one in the shop.

'We got some like that at home only better'

To the untrained eye, the piece of china in the shop, which happens to be by a major maker and in perfect condition with a price tag of hundreds of pounds, may well seem to be identical to the copy worth £20 that the person has at home. Very often, the reverse applies and the customer concerned sees a damaged item at £50 and assumes that their perfect copy is worth the same.

In either case, there would be no problem if the person concerned would only talk to the dealer, instead of rejecting his or her offers of help with a silly 'just looking' and going away with the wrong idea as to their item's identity and worth.

Again, I advise common sense. If you see an item marked at £100 in a shop then it must follow that it's not worth that. If it were, it would not still be in the shop.

10

The Dealer's View

I was standing one day with an old trade buddy of mine, look-ing out of the window of my shop at the world going by, when he suddenly commented, 'You know, Rothery, all those people out there are, for the most part, decent types. They love their old mums, are kind to their children, pay their taxes and give freely to charity. Why is it the moment they enter shops like ours, they turn into such monsters?'

My mind immediately went to the occasion when I had seen, just inside an antiques shop, a box on which was writ-ten in large letters 'BRAIN PARK'. Both unkind and unfair to the majority of collectors but, sadly, with an underlying truth, because a great many people do let their enthusiasm get the better of both their innate good manners and common sense when in antiques shops and behave in a most strange and unfortunate manner. They become, in turn, aggressive, defensive, rude and even downright silly. The saddest thing of all is they do not know they are doing it.

Not, of course dear reader, that I am for one minute sug-gesting that you are one of these people. But, the illustrative stories that I tell might remind you of someone who is and to whom, in the spirit of friendship, you may choose to pass on the advice and guidance I give in this book. Unlikely as it may seem, you might possibly recognise some of your own peccadilloes and learn something to your advantage.

I think the main problem stems from the inability of

collectors to understand that antiques shops are businesses and run as such. Unfortunately, some shop owners have the same problem.

This attitude was brought home to me one day when, during a conversation with a collector who was also a highly qualified accountant, the subject turned to business matters and the problems of running a small business. I was cheerfully discussing cash flow, retained profit ratios, annual returns on investment etc. when I realised he was looking at me rather quizzically. I asked him if I had said something wrong. He smiled and said, 'No, but one does not expect antiques dealers to talk business matters in the way you just have.' I asked him why not since surely these were the very things that he, as an accountant, was constantly trying to ram home to his business clients. He laughed and said, 'You are absolutely right, of course, but being a collector, even though I am also an accountant, I suppose that in my enthusiasm for antiques I forget that yours is a serious business just like any other.'

This gentleman is not alone in his view of the antiques business, indeed his, it seems, is the generally held view of most collectors.

Without, I hope, causing offence, let me make it crystal clear to you that antiques dealers are people who, like you, are doing a job to the best of their ability in the hope of a decent wage from which they can pay their mortgage, educate their children and buy the new kitchen that their wives have been nagging them about.

Again, just like you, in their young days they struggled to get by on a pittance while they studied and learnt their profession. Then, as they have gleaned experience, they have climbed their own professional ladder to where they are today in exactly the same way as you have. They will, in the main, try to do a good job for you as you would for your clients. All they ask is that you show them the same professional courtesy, as you would expect to be shown to you. Once, having put this to a client, he looked me up and down and said, 'Yes, but you are only a dealer.' I really did not know whether to hit him or admire him. He was, after all, only saying outright what a lot of collectors indicate by their attitudes and body language.

None of the above, of course, applies to the 'boot sale' bandits or 'the fairies' of the fairs.

Surely people in the antiques trade do it because they enjoy it?

Sure they do. Don't you enjoy your job?

One of the most widely held misconceptions is that the antiques dealer is a fellow collector. Most professionals are not and those that do invariably collect something different to what they are dealing in as an everyday business. My old friend Dave Crabtree, when asked what he collected, would invariably reply 'Money!' I have never collected anything, even as a child.

If anyone reading this ever tries for a job in the trade with a proper dealer, for goodness sake do not tell them you are a collector. If you do, you will kill your chances stone dead. The last thing any properly run business wants is someone behind the counter who spends over much time with clients with the same interests and either ignores, or worse, rubbishes anyone or anything that is not in their particular field. What is worse, the enthusiast will want to reserve every decent bit that comes in, either for themselves or their friends.

One of the few sensible remarks members of the public make in shops is, 'I couldn't do your job. I would want to take everything home.'

A small point here that might amuse you is the fact that, at 5.30, the shop people heave a sigh of relief when they put up the 'Closed' sign, in the same way as any other workers do. They also tell terrible fibs when they go out socially if asked about what they do as a living, usually claiming to be in some mundane occupation or another and thus avoiding getting their ear bent talking shop to an over-enthusiastic collector. Very much like you and me, they would rather concentrate their attention on the food, the drink and that very attractive person who has just entered the room.

Part of the odd behaviour of collectors in shops is that, as soon as they open their mouths, they appear to speak in strange and foreign tongues, with little or no resemblance to English. 'Wot you got on that, mate?' evidently means, 'How much is that item, please?' 'Wot's your best, mate?' means 'Are you prepared to negotiate?' 'I collect blue and white.' Blue and white what, for goodness sake?

The twee brigade give themselves grandiose titles which they have difficulty in pronouncing, do not understand and which, in some cases, cannot be found in any dictionary. Here are a few examples:

Phalaristics	the collecting of cloth badges
Digitologist	collector of thimbles
Arctophiles	collectors of teddy bears
Tegestollogist	collector of beer mats
Cartophillist	collector of cigarette cards
Phillumenast	collector of matchboxes
Deltiologist	collector of postcards
Treenologist	objects made of wood

The use of 'in words' is nothing new. In my early days effete young men would fling back their hair and lisp that they were looking for '*object d'art*' or '*objects d'virtue*' (how very much nicer than smalls), and I actually took cover behind the desk when a large mustachioed, tweed clad lady boomed at me that she was looking for 'Mary Gregory'.

The purpose of all this silly talk is, I am told by a psychiatrist, to establish to anyone in earshot that the person concerned is a member of the 'in crowd' and to establish their credibility among the *cognoscente*. The use of in-words and collectors' slang in a shop usually only establishes to the dealer the fact that they have a plonker on their hands.

This need to be recognised as a fellow expert is also manifested by strange actions and rituals often involving little bits of accoutra, which some people carry almost as a badge rather than a tool. Watch as the furniture buff produces his or her own pocket tape-measure or the silver buff their personal magnifying glass and book of assay marks. Other items of witchcraft include magnets, small torches, pocket guidebooks and small cameras. Many enthusiasts, with or without the aid of the aforementioned items, then proceed to make themselves look totally ridiculous by indulging in weird and wonderful rituals.

Shotgun shooters look up the barrels of guns from the wrong direction, simulate mounting and swinging the gun and finally hold the butt of the gun in the crook of their arm and stretch their forearm along the stock. They mostly have no idea why they do this other than they have seen other people do it. Motor enthusiasts love kicking the tyres of the cars they are looking at or grasping the front wheel and shaking it. All this serves no other purpose than to alert the dealer to the fact that they have yet another nutter on their hands.

With regards to this 'Look at me, I'm an expert!' syndrome and its use in the antiques world, allow me to illustrate. My good friend David, if asked if an object was silver, would breathe heavily on it, rub it furiously with his sleeve, then sniff it. You could always tell if a client had been in David's shop, as they would all follow the same procedure in other shops much to the amusement of the shopkeepers.

Once, having explained at great length the various points about a certain knife to a client, he asked me for the umpteenth time if it was genuine. Holding it lightly between my thumb and forefinger, I struck the blade sharply on the counter, then held it to my ear as if listening, rather as one would use a tuning-fork. Then, straight-faced, I pronounced it as genuine.

The client was very impressed with this display of trade 'know-how' and departed.

A fellow dealer who was something of a specialist on this type of knife and had heard the conversation and, while agreeing with all I had said, asked me what the tuning-fork business was all about. I told him absolutely nothing but that I would bet him that before the month was out, all the half-hard experts at the militaria fairs would be practising the same ritual. I won my bet with a week to spare!

Another manifestation of this need to be recognised as an established collector or dealer and part of the in-crowd, is the unpleasant habit of name-dropping. Many times I have had someone come into the shop and, within a few minutes, they have mentioned half a dozen names, most of which I have never heard of. On the rare occasions when I do recognise a name and mention to that person that I had a friend or client of theirs in, the reaction is invariably, 'Who?' and then after I have described the person, 'Oh, that twit!'

Many a time I have been in company where one of these idiots has gone on at great length about their friendship with some well-known dealer or another, not knowing that their so-called pal is actually sitting opposite them. Somebody once said that it is better to stay silent and appear to be a fool than to open your mouth and prove it.

Believe me, dear reader, no real collector like you needs to be part of any in-crowd or to adopt their strange jargon or even stranger rituals.

Here is another of those crazy conversations that crop up about three times a week.

'I have got a Nagasaki bus stop.'
'That's nice.'
'I'll bring it in for you to look at.'
'Great. How much do you want for it?'
'I don't want to sell it.'
'I see, you want a valuation. No problem.'

'No, I don't want a valuation.'

'Well, why are you going to bring it in?'

'For you to look at.'

'Sir, if you don't want to sell it or have a valuation, what on earth is the point of you bringing it in?'

'For you to look at.'

'Why, sir, should I want to look at it?'

'So you can see it.'

'Sir, this is a shop. We buy, sell and value objects. We do not look at them.'

'Don't you want to look at my Nagasaki bus stop then?'

'With the greatest of respect, sir, if you ever wish to sell it or have it valued, I would be delighted to help you, but there really is no point in my just looking at it.'

'Well, in that case, I won't bring it in for you to look at.'

The proud owner leaves, somewhat miffed, and the dealer bangs his head against the wall.

We all of us make mistakes and are sometimes guilty of committing, unintentionally and sometimes with misplaced good intent, the most awful gaffes. This is never more so than in collectors' shops. I am fully aware that you are a very nice person and would never ever intentionally be rude or unkind to anyone. Nor would you wish to appear stupid, which is why I am trying to warn you of the pitfalls that sometimes lie in the collector's path.

Before agreeing to write this book, I talked to dozens of professional dealers who complained of the strange and hurtful things that collectors do without realising it. I asked some of them why they didn't say something at the time and got the daft answer, 'Well, we didn't like to, but you can put it in your book.' They then proceeded to tell me the latest horror story that has befallen them. One book dealer actually showed me a book of stupid remarks that book collectors made. It was called *Bookworm Droppings*. I'd love to meet the author, just to shake his or her hand, not least because every single one of those inane comments could have been made about silver, jewellery, furniture or any other collectable.

I do most sincerely ask you to believe that I am not telling you these tales for any other reason than that I have seen too many good relationships lost by some thoughtless comment by collectors and, indeed, by snappy smart-arse retorts by dealers.

You have, or will have one day, a very nice collection of which you are rightfully proud. You've worked hard to build it up, done overtime or forgone other pleasures to pay for it. All in all, big or small, you are rather proud of it, and quite rightly so.

You have given much thought as to how you should display it to advantage. You then invite a guest to view your lovely collection. What is your reaction if that guest then proceeds to find fault with every bit of it and takes a perverse delight in pointing out to you every little defect, which you already know about, then generally rubbishes all your hard work and effort?

You would most certainly be justifiably tempted to show them the door and, quite rightly, most collectors would feel the same. So why do so many collectors do exactly that in the dealer's shop?

One young man who, I am pleased to say, is one of my star collectors, did, in his foolish youth, do just that. He inspected an item closely and then, in the full bloom of his 19 years he gave me a lecture all about it and proceeded to find fault with every little bit. Finally, with the smug look that know-alls effect, he handed it back to me. I put it back in the cabinet.

'Just a minute, I want that,' he expostulated.

'No, young sir. If it were as bad as you've just pointed out, I would feel guilty selling it to you. Why don't you come back when I've got a better one and you've got rather more money?'

He never ever again rubbished other people's goods and has become a very nice young man and a serious collector.

What on earth is it about quite a few collectors that makes them think that shopkeepers hide things away? Not satisfied with such inane questions like, 'What have you got hidden away?', or 'You haven't anything out the back, have you?', they then attempt a covert search of the establishment. Every attempt to help them is answered by this damn silly 'Just looking'. At the same time, they indulge in the most amazing antics, such as dropping their car keys on the floor and, while picking them up, taking a long hard look under the counters and desks to see what might be lurking there. The way they contort their necks trying to squint round doors and corners sometimes makes me fear that they might do themselves an injury.

The dealer, of course, can always brighten an otherwise dreary afternoon by putting an empty box in the corner and covering it with a piece of old cloth, then watch these fools, amid countless protestations of 'just looking', sidle towards it and hover by it until they think the staff are not looking.

Then, when they surreptitiously lift the cloth and peek inside, the cloth is rapidly dropped when an icy voice enquires, 'Are you sure there is nothing you are looking for, sir?'

We did have a variation of this game where we put in the box a stuffed '*Penis giganticus*' from some poor old elephant, but had to stop doing it when several ladies and a couple of strange blokes tried to pinch it.

The common sense answer is that, since the dealer is there to sell goods and make a living, they are hardly likely to lessen their chances of doing both by hiding goods away. Skipper, as we have read, played on this syndrome and allowed people to find the swords and to pay twice as much as the going price for the pleasure of doing so. There are some dealers at the bottom end of all fields of collecting who constantly do the same.

One of the worst examples of bad behaviour brought on by

over-enthusiasm, which is sadly very common, is the tendency for people to butt into conversations that the dealer is having with another client. This is especially galling if someone brings something in to sell or have valued and another person in the shop moves in and starts picking up the items concerned at the same time, commenting on them and offering uninvited, unwanted and invariably inaccurate advice.

Nothing annoys a dealer more than when a collector tries to use the shop as a meeting place to contact other collectors. Some even have the barefaced audacity to demand pen and paper so they might exchange names and addresses. Think about it. The dealer is trying to make a living. The last thing they want is for collectors to meet and sell or exchange directly with each other, cutting them out in the process, let alone having the cheek to use their shop to do it.

In a similar vein, and equally annoying, is the interfering sod who thinks they are being helpful: when they hear the dealer tell someone that they do not at the moment have the thing they are looking for, they barge into the conversation with, 'Joe Smith has got one of those.' They then go on to give detailed instructions about how to find Mr Smith's shop, sometimes even asking for pen and paper to draw a map. It never occurs to them that the shopkeeper has the item coming in next week which they can then sell to the person concerned, let alone the fact that not only have they lost the poor shop-keeper a much-needed sale, they have introduced the client to the competition. Such actions will not endear them to the dealer. When people like this are taken to task the invariable answer is, 'I didn't think of it like that. I was only trying to be helpful.' To whom? Most certainly not the dealer.

Would you believe that on many occasions I have had people actually try to push in and try to buy an item that I was being offered in the shop. Sometimes when a client has over-heard me refuse an item, they have admonished me with, 'Why on earth didn't you buy that? You know, I would have been interested.' They do not, as a rule, pursue the matter when they see me pick up the phone and hear me inform the dealer squad that one of the stolen pieces they have been looking for has just been offered to me.

The all-time classic must be the occasion when I was visiting a friend's shop. A gentleman who was obviously a regular client there came in bubbling with enthusiasm, to announce that he and some other enthusiasts had got together and were to hold a swap meeting in the local town hall. He produced a large poster, which read something like:

Collectors Swap Meeting
Town hall: Fifteen stalls
Open to buy, sell and exchange

It did, of course, also give times and dates etc. Not noticing the stony look that had appeared on the dealer's face, he then asked the dealer to put the poster in a prominent place in his window. I was lost with admiration as the dealer, with great dignity and superb self-control, explained quietly and politely that his window was for the purpose of displaying his goods in the hope of selling them. He continued that if any passers by or visitors to his shop did have items which they wished to 'sell, buy or exchange', he felt disinclined to suggest that they went elsewhere with them. He also expressed his sadness that, having helped and advised these collectors over many years, they should now thank him by setting up in competition.

One thoroughly obnoxious and slimy specimen, who I had been trying to get rid of for ages, made a habit of listening to what was going on in the shop and following people out to introduce himself and to try to buy what they had. One day, I refused an item and watched as he hurried down the road after the guy. Money and goods changed hands. Next time he came in I greeted him like a long lost brother. 'Ah, just the man I

153

wanted to see. Do you remember that guy last week that was trying to sell me a Nagasaki bus stop? Only the police came in soon after looking for him. Evidently he had been involved in an aggravated burglary where someone got badly hurt. I noticed you went out about the same time and wondered if you had seen what sort of car he got into. I told them you wouldn't mind helping.'

I excused myself to attend to another customer and when I looked round he had gone. Funny thing, he never did come back.

There is one behaviour pattern that some collectors indulge in that really annoys me and that is when someone who has only just met me wants to be my bosom pal. They affect the false ingratiating smile that politicians adopt and gooily simper '. . . and what do I call you?'

Normally, I fix them with the same stare that my old sergeant major used on us young gentlemen when we got out of line, and tell them, 'You call me Mr Rothery and I call you sir.'

In my opinion, a shop is a place of business and not some sort of social club. Good manners and service should be expected and received. Over-familiarity is not acceptable.

One visitor to the shop commented on the fact that even my longest-standing customers called me Mr Rothery and I returned the compliment. I explained to him that the use of my Christian name was a privilege extended only to my family and close friends and that I avoided getting on first name terms with customers in case I mistook this as a sign of personal friendship. I might start to expect all sorts of privileges, such as them paying me more than I was asking and only dealing with me, and even letting me owe them money or, more likely and more dangerously, the reverse might be presumed.

A client once pointed out to me that in all American businesses and even in the Cabinet Room of Number Ten, the use of forenames was the norm. As I told him, I would prefer not to get down to that level.

Once, having explained the above to a customer, another client who was in the shop and had overheard the conversation grinned broadly and, when we were alone, commented that in his barber's shop the same procedure existed. When he had asked his barber why, after 30 years, he still called his clients Mr, the old boy replied ''Cos I don't want to know the bastards.'

There have evidently been plonkers on the fringe of the trade since time immemorial. Then, as now, they made the same silly, obvious observations, such as drawing the dealer's notice to faults that the dealer is perfectly aware of, or telling the dealer all about their various items of stock of which they are equally aware. The favourite comment is, 'It's very nice, shame you haven't got the other one. A pair would be much more valuable.' As if the dealer didn't already know that. Sometimes the dealer would agree with them, then produce the other one and invite them to buy the pair. They rarely did.

A very old story that was doing the rounds when I first started concerned a pair of vases. Evidently, the local TFI of the time spotted a rather nice vase in a shop priced at £50. He took the trouble to explain to the very experienced dealer that a pair like it would probably be worth £200. The dealer had the temerity to disagree with him and explained that he knew that his vase was one of a pair because when he bought it the vendor had told him that an uncle had given him and his brother one each. Unfortunately, the brother's one had been sold some months previous.

The dealer then told TFI that, in his opinion, should the missing vase ever come to light, he would value it at £200 alone and, reunited with its twin, it would, in his view, make the pair worth something like £400. As with most of his ilk, the TFI travelled great distances in his constant search for something for nothing and when, in the far north of the county, he visited the premises of Mr Jones, to his delight, he spotted the twin to the vase he had seen earlier. It was marked up at

£150, which he explained to Mr Jones was far too much for a singleton. Mr Jones agreed but told him a very similar story about the two brothers and expressed the opinion that the other vase must be somewhere in the county and whoever found it would have a pair worth over £400. A deal was struck at £140. The vase, carefully wrapped, was put in the back of the car, which TFI drove rapidly back to the first dealer. After the usual small talk, TFI casually brought up the question of the vase that he had seen some time previously. 'Sorry,' said the dealer. 'I sold that last week to Mr Jones.'

You know, dear reader, when you hear stories like that, it renews one's faith in the existence of a good and just God.

Proper dealers do not, as a rule, conspire together for the purpose of putting one over on the public. They are, however, sometimes obliged, as a form of mutual protection, to work very closely together, especially when some sly member of the public is trying to put one over on them. For some strange reason, the collectors assume that the dealers do not know each other or that they do, but hate each other's guts. Let me explain to you how it really works in practice. Originally, some 40 years ago, there were three of us. Dave Crabtree, Peter Hancock and I. Sadly, dear old Dave is no longer with us, but Peter is still going strong. We had very little capital between us and were, on occasion, obliged to combine our funds to buy the odd collection. Over the years, we each of us became established in our different ways, but maintained a deep and abiding relationship which enabled us to work together when the situation demanded.

The unwritten rules were quite simple. We were in competition, so it was perfectly right and proper to pull strokes on each other or to outwit each other in any business deals, sometimes one getting the better on a deal, sometimes vice versa. Occasionally, we all got too clever between us and completely cocked up a deal so that we all lost out. After 40 years I would like to think that the score sheet showed a draw.

When it came to the less pleasant members of the public or the jackals that lurk on the fringe of the trade masquerading as dealers trying to see any one or all of us off, then we would work as one to ensure that not only were their devious plans thwarted, but that, if possible, we gave them a bloody nose into the bargain.

Here are a few illustrations of how it really works.

Sweet old lady comes into shop and, from the ubiquitous plastic bag, produces a Nagasaki bus stop.

'I don't know what this is but would you be interested in buying it?'

'Certainly, madam, how much do you want for it?'

'I've no idea what it is'

157

'Like I said,' she whines, 'I don't even know what it is, let alone what it's worth.'

'Well madam, it's exactly what Mr Crabtree told you when you took it in this morning, but now it's worth less than he offered you.'

If one connects the old harridan with some brain picker that has been banned from the premises, there might be added, 'and remind your blue-rinse friend that neither Mr Crabtree nor I are here to price stuff up for her stall at the Hotel Plastico tomorrow.'

It might be the awful knocker boy: ''Ere, Mr Roffry. I got a good bit of gear 'ere. You're the only one oos seen it, 'cos I knows you'll give me a fair price. Wots it worf?'

As a result of several phone calls received earlier in the day, one immediately recognises the proffered item and offers, tongue in cheek, £50.

'Nah, I give more than that.' They always have. 'Anyway, Mr Crabtree offered me £100.'

'I thought you said no one had seen it?'

'On my baby's life, only Mr Crabtree.'

'Much as I fear for the health and well-being of that poor child of yours, you're a bloody liar. You've shown it to several people and Mr Crabtree offered you £40 for it. Now push off. I don't want it at any price, and, by the way, neither does Mr Crabtree.'

On one amazing occasion, rather similar to the one above, I was completely taken aback when, after my having accused the guy of not telling the truth, he replied, completely unabashed, 'Yeah, I know I'm a knocker boy, ain't I? We always tell lies, that's how we make a living, innit?'

The following saga is one of the all-time greats. It should be recounted to the children of established dealers on their fathers' knees. It illustrates how two of history's most obnoxious, lying TFIs both got their just desserts within a month and with one and the same item.

The first of our villains, despite his unpleasant ways, was tolerated by the trade because he occasionally came up with the odd nice piece. The problem was that, on the rare occasions this happened, he would hawk the piece round and round the trade until we all got thoroughly cheesed off with both it and him. In the process, he would promise the same item to several dealers in return for their having helped him with information and advice on the item. One day, our hero(?) got his hands on a rather desirable pistol. He showed it to dealer one who offered him £200 for it. He accepted the offer but asked if he could keep the pistol for a while to do some research on it. Dealer one agreed but, knowing this chap as he did, only on the condition that it was not, under any circumstances, to be shown (let alone offered) to any other member of the trade. This was agreed. In conversation with another trade member a few days later, it became apparent that almost the same deal had been struck with dealer two. Further investigation revealed the same deal again with dealer three.

We now had three rather unhappy dealers, intent on wreaking revenge on the awful TFI. Breaking his legs was the favourite option but was generally felt to be a trifle extreme. Banning him from all three shops was the obvious option but this would have put him out of reach of any retribution that might be meted out to him. A plan was hatched.

That evening, TFI got a phone call from dealer one, who was most insistent that the agreed deal should be rapidly concluded. The suggestion was made that to speed things up he was prepared to come round to the house immediately to collect the pistol and, as a gesture of goodwill, pay an extra £50. Hiding behind the usual lie of 'I'll think about it,' TFI declined.

A little later that same evening, dealer two phoned and, after some casual chit-chat, raised the question of the pistol. He also raised his offer. By now, TFI was getting the feeling that the sudden anxiety of the first two dealers to get their hands on the thing might suggest that it was worth a lot more money than was first thought. His little greed buds going nineteen to the dozen, he spent a sleepless night.

Early next morning, he was onto dealer three. After the usual small talk, he broached the subject of the pistol. Dealer three hesitated for some time, then ruefully admitted that, having further researched the pistol in depth, he was now of the opinion that it could be a very rare type worth thousands of pounds. As such, of course, it was way out of his league and he suggested that the only place to sell it could be the London auctions. So the TFI took a day off and the early morning train to London, where he was in the fond hope that he was about to make a fortune. He was more than a little surprised when his suggestion that he had a rare and valuable pistol caused great mirth to all who saw it and was equally surprised to be told that, after fees, he would be lucky to see back £150. A much chastened and wiser man boarded the train home that night, but before the train reached Guildford, his mood brightened as he had had a good idea, or so he thought.

The following day, he phoned dealer three and pointed out that, in view of his honesty, he could have the pistol for only £500. Dealer three explained that, although touched by this guy's kind offer, he had done even more research which showed, to his embarrassment, that his assessment of the pistol had been completely wrong. The item in question was the most common model in existence and therefore he would prefer not to buy it.

TFI phoned dealer two and got exactly the same response. Finally, he visited dealer one and reluctantly agreed to accept his offer of £250. Dealer one told him, in no uncertain terms, that as the pistol had been offered to all and sundry, contrary to the original arrangement, he didn't want it either.

The pistol finally changed hands when dealer one relented and finally did agree to buy it for £150. That particular person, as with all his ilk, eventually faded from the collecting scene, unmissed and unlamented.

Part two of the saga commenced when dealer one, having acquired the pistol, marked it up at a very reasonable £225 and put it in his window. It should be noted for reasons that will become clear later, that this particular dealer invariably tucked the price tags of the items in the window under the items concerned, so that they could not be read from outside.

There was at this time another devout brain-picker and liar who, for the purpose of this story, we shall call TFI two. Also at this period, I rather foolishly allowed my private telephone number and address to be published in the local directory. The result was that I would get calls at all sorts of inconvenient times from over-enthusiastic collectors who evidently thought that dealers were not entitled to any degree of privacy.

TFI two brought this particular form of gratuitous intrusion to a fine art. Evenings and weekends he would phone me to pick my brains, eventually calling on me at my home unannounced, usually just as we were sitting down to dinner with guests and, on one famous occasion, at lunchtime on Christmas day.

On reading the above, my much-loved regular clients and dear friends in the trade will at last understand why I am ex-directory and have steadfastly refused to give them my private number or tell them where I live.

The situation was evidently that TFI two's wife had relatives in Cosham. He would bring her over on Sundays and bank holidays, leave her with her relatives and spend the day looking in the antiques shop windows in the Portsmouth area. In the event that he spotted anything, he would hammer on the side door of the poor shopkeepers that lived above the premises or take full advantage of the invitation, 'When closed, phone ------' that some dealers were silly enough to put in their windows.

The stage is then set for the second part of the saga.

Sunday lunch was again disturbed by TFI two who described, in great detail, a pistol he had come across. His description was so accurate that I immediately recognised it as '*that*' pistol which I knew to be in dealer one's window. Feigning great interest, I asked if it was in the Portsmouth area. He, lying through his teeth as usual, assured me that in fact it was down in Dorset. Guessing what he was up to, I made it clear to him that, in my opinion, he had chanced across a highly desirable find that could be worth as much as £600.

He assured me that should he be fortunate enough to acquire the item I would be the first to know and, in view of our friendship, he would only want a small profit to cover his expenses.

As soon as he was off the phone, I called my friend, explained the situation and suggested that if the TFI did contact him, he should ask £475 and come down to £400. This he readily agreed to as he too had a few scores to settle with this particular Herbert. I then returned to a cold Sunday lunch and an irate wife.

Just after tea, my buddy called back. He could hardly speak for laughing as he recounted how, a few minutes after I had rung off, TFI two had called from a public call box and explained that he was only in Portsmouth for the day and desperately wanted to see the pistol in the window. To this end, would the proprietor leave his lunch and drive several miles to open up the shop for him to have a look at it. My friend explained that he had no intention of forgoing his Sunday lunch and travelling all that way on the off chance of a sale but, on the clear understanding that the guy was serious and accepted the price of £475 he would meet him outside the shop in a couple of hours.

This TFI two agreed to.

On arrival at the shop, it was explained to the client that he would have to wait outside for a few minutes while the shop owner switched off the alarms. The shop owner entered the premises and, pausing only to snatch the pistol from the window, disappeared to the back of the shop, ostensibly to switch off the alarms but in fact to remove the label showing £225.

Despite what he had agreed on the phone, as soon as TFI two got his hands on the item, he exhibited all his usual nasty little traits by finding all sorts of non-existent faults, and then started haggling. Notwithstanding this, a deal was agreed and – at this stage my friend almost choked with laughter – at £425.

When we both finally settled down and stopped giggling, it was agreed that £200 as the original trade price, plus the odd £25 for turning out on a Sunday, should go to dealer one as of right, and the remaining £200 be divided between us. My £100 went to Dr Barnardo's and his to another charity.

As soon as I could on the Monday, I phoned the new owner of the pistol at his place of work in Weymouth to ask anxiously if he had managed to obtain the item that we had talked about the day before. He informed me not yet but not to worry, if he did get it I should be the first to know.

Over the next several weeks, I received calls from as far away as Berty in Cornwall and Allan Lincoln in London, plus a few in between telling me that TFI two had got hold of rather a nice pistol but was asking a crazy price for it, even by his standards. Some were asking, did I think that he had finally flipped? Each enquirer was made privy to what had happened and allowed to share the enjoyment. The usual comment being that it could not have happened to a better guy.

A few Sunday mornings later, the horrible little man phoned me with the news that he had finally managed, only the previous night, to obtain that pistol we had talked about and he had made a special trip down to sell it to me. Unfortunately, the owner had proved rather difficult and he had had to pay the full £600 that I had originally offered and, what with the extra expenses, it would have to cost me £650. I pointed out that I had not offered him that much, but had only expressed the opinion that it might be worth that much. He was, however, most welcome to come round after lunch but not during.

Late afternoon, and he arrived and gently unwrapped the pistol. Panting with greed, he stood back and awaited my reaction.

'Good lord, that's the old beast that dealer one had in his window for ages and nobody wanted. Who stuffed you up with that?!'

This unpleasant specimen also eventually faded away, unwept, unhonoured and unsung.

I have, at great length, explained to you the differences between the various types of dealer but, it must be said that we in the trade are sometimes guilty, especially after a bad day, of forgetting all the nice people we've dealt with, like you, dear reader, and only remembering the horrors. 'The bloody public' as we quite unfairly call them.

Many is the dealer's wife who, on his return, asks what sort of a day has he had only to hear, 'Bloody collectors, they're driving me up the wall.'

Portsmouth is the UK home of IBM, the famous computer company. I was slightly involved in bringing them here and very welcome they have been, bringing jobs to the area and extra prosperity. But where, oh where, do they get their staff from?

There is a well-held theory among Portsmouth traders that IBM stands for 'I'm bloody marvellous'. The majority, when in shops, are time-wasting, arrogant, self-opinionated nitwits. So much so that any unpleasant customer is now automatically known as an IBMer.

The answer to 'How's it gone today, Bert?' might well be 'Awful: bloody IBMers all day!'

I was dining one night with one of IBM's senior directors and raised the matter with him. He smiled. 'They are nice ordinary people when we recruit them, but we train them up to believe that they're working for the greatest company in the world and that we only employ the best. They don't just think they're the cat's whiskers, they know it. What are you moaning about anyway? You only see them occasionally, I have to put up with them all day!'

What on earth has this got to do with collecting? I'll tell you.

The TFIs, IBMers, association officers and other clever dicks never get the best out of the trade who will, in extreme cases, go out of their way to trip them up and ensure that whatever they want is never available. Hence, I have tried to warn you how to avoid being included in these groups, to the detriment of your collecting career.

An example of the dealer's revenge.

One of our regulars likes to be left alone to select his purchases. As he selects each item, he puts it on the counter, and so on until he has a pile of goods to his satisfaction. One piece he chose was removed from his pile and returned to the rack from whence it came. He looked confused, retrieved it from the rack and re-added it to his pile. Again, it was removed and returned to the rack. Somewhat exasperated, he informed me, 'I want that item, Mr Rothery.'

'No, you don't, sir.' I gently informed him.

'Yes, I do.' Then the penny dropped. 'Why don't I want that item?' he asked.

'Because it's a complete fake. You should have known from the price, which is about a quarter of what it should be, as you well know.' Somewhat sheepishly, he admitted that he had thought I'd made a mistake and that he ought to have known better.

As we are settling up for his purchases and wrapping them, in walks TFI. 'What old tat have you today?' he bellows, completely ignoring the fact that I have a client with me. I wish him good morning and carry on with my client. TFI walks straight up to the rack, grabs the item we had just been talking about and returns to the counter. He pushes his way in front of the client with whom I am dealing and says, 'I know you're too tight-fisted to haggle, here's your money!' And, having thrown the money down, he walks out.

I apologise to the client for the oaf's bad behaviour. The client, slightly bemused, says, 'Mr Rothery, you have just warned me against that item and now you have sold it to him.'

'No, sir,' I explain. 'Had he asked me, I would have told him, but he didn't, because, like you, he thought I had made a mistake in the price. Unlike you, he is not a valued customer in this establishment so I let him buy it, but I didn't sell it to him.'

One horror operated around Salisbury, constantly picking people's brains and asking dealers to hold goods for ages and then changing his mind. He also promised several dealers the same goods but never kept his word. He finally got his come-uppance in Tony Earle's shop. I had been to the West Country and bought an important collection of Georgian swords. As usual, I stopped at Tony's on the way back and he asked to see them, so I took them into his back room.

As we were looking at them, in walked, unannounced and uninvited, this Wiltshire horror. His eyes alighted on about £2,000 worth of super swords but, before he could open his mouth, I said, 'OK then, Mr Earle, that's a deal.' Dear old Tony cottoned on straight away and played along. I carefully counted out £200 on Tony's table and, having done so, asked him to give me a hand putting my purchases in the car. We even pressed the horror into helping to carry them out. An hour or so later, I phoned Tony to see if chummy had gone and went back and collected my £200.

Years later, long after Tony had died, I met a guy who told me that he had an acquaintance near Salisbury who often told him how he had just missed a magnificent collection of swords

166

by a couple of minutes because some fly dealer from Portsmouth had got there first.

Tony would have enjoyed that.

'I will never come into this shop again!' is a threat that many collectors think strikes fear into the hearts of all dealers. Be careful if you use it, the answer may be a softly spoken, but heartfelt 'Thank you'.

Most proper dealers are, of course, most hurt and upset when they fall out with a good customer. Apart from the bad feeling, it is not good for business to lose regular customers. There are, however, a few, a very few, who can, by their behaviour, upset not only the proprietor but also other customers and thus poison the whole atmosphere of an establishment. The dealer cannot give way to bullying and hectoring under the threat of boycott by these few. In fact, it is, in all probability, good business to keep them out of the shop in the interests of other customers. When a local club secretary, who was being a thorough nuisance and annoying everyone in the shop, would not leave when asked, one of my female staff was obliged, sadly, to put an armlock on him and physically eject him. Her action was greeted with a warm round of applause from the other customers.

I was in one shop when a particularly unpleasant lady was trying to bully the owner, telling him that unless he conceded to her demands she would have to consider going elsewhere, when he stopped her in her tracks with, 'Madam, what is your favourite charity?' At her reply of, 'Well, I support several,' he told her, 'Madam, I am prepared to give £5 a week to any charity you care to nominate on condition that you stay out of my shop!'

On the question of telephones – they are both a blessing and a curse in the antiques shop. Dear old ladies will insist on phoning up to ask long, involved questions about items they have and seem incapable of understanding that the dealer can neither identify nor value them without seeing the items. If the dealer tries to shorten the call by explaining, most politely, that they have a shop full of people to serve, they can get rather shirty.

One, in great dudgeon, once said to me, 'Well, if you think doing business is more important than helping me, I won't bother in future.'

So, if you do need to call your dealer on a Saturday morning when you know they are busy, do ask if it's convenient to talk and offer to call back later if it is not. They will almost certainly be willing to call you back when things have quietened down if you asked them.

I think I shall say no more other than: the next time some flash poser disturbs the smooth running of my establishment with a rendering of Colonel Bogie on their mobile phone, I shall probably shoot them. Please switch the beastly things off when you go into a shop or, better still, leave them in the car.

Scenario 1

Monday morning and the dealer has just opened the mail to be faced with a final demand for business rates and numerous other bills. Enter the collector. 'I bought this at a boot sale yesterday and want to know all about it and whether I paid the right money for it.'

Dear and gentle reader, the last thing the dealer wants to hear is that you have spent your money elsewhere, and they are unlikely to tell you what a clever little collector you are for doing so.

Scenario 2

Collector standing in shop surrounded by antiques on all sides. 'Do you buy antiques?'

Scenario 3

Very posh antiques shop, full of lovely but expensive items with proprietor and fellow dealer talking quietly on raised bit at the end. Enter two 'ladies'. Tweed skirts, Jaeger sweaters, Cyro pearls round their necks. In voices raised several decibels to ensure they are heard, they commence a conversation.

'Isn't that awful. We had one but threw it out and just look at the price on that. Wouldn't give it house room.'

They continue in the same vein for some time and then, having been offensive about everything in the place, go quiet. At this moment the proprietor turns to his visitor and, in a voice that would have carried across the Albert Hall, comments, 'I say Jones, look at that woman's bloody awful outfit.'

I once watched a very knowledgeable dealer flogging his guts out for ages trying to help and advise a rather morose collector who, when he left the building, muttered over his shoulder a grudging, 'Thanks.' When I asked him why on earth we bothered with some of them, he replied, 'Mr Rothery, doing a good job for the collectors is like peeing yourself in a dark suit. You get a warm feeling but nobody notices!'

Do not ask that well-known silly question, 'Where did you get that?' or 'Where do you get your stock from?' You will, in all probability, get an equally silly answer, such as Dave Crabtree's standard reply of 'I stole it off an old lady!' or mine of 'If you leave them in the dark overnight, they breed.' Don't be daft! No dealer in his or her right mind is going to tell you. If you knew, you would go direct and the dealer would lose their livelihood.

Here's a bit of good advice that it saddens me deeply to have to give you but you should know. When you get a slice of good luck and find something nice at a very favourable price, by all means tell your wife or husband or any friends who are neither dealers nor collectors but do not boast about it, either to your tame dealer or your fellow collectors. Neither will feel pleased at your good fortune. In fact, they will resent it. The dealer because it is another deal they have missed, and the collector because they are envious. The more times you do it, the more they will hate you for it, so keep your good fortune to yourself.

Here's another situation that you might find hard to believe.

'I am thinking of opening a shop like yours but none of the dealers are being very helpful. They refuse to tell me where to get stock and won't let me introduce myself to the other customers in their shops. I really don't know how to get started. What would be your advice, Mr Rothery'

'Don't, sunshine. Not on my bloody patch!'

It has happened to me more than once.

The other daft question is: 'Are there any other shops like yours in the area?' Many people seem to think that we are all chums and that the business side of the trade is as big a game as collecting. It is not a game. It is a highly competitive business where people are working long and hard to make a living for themselves and their families. No professional businessman or woman is going to knock the competition but they are most certainly not going to help them by recommending them to their customers.

If you go to a silversmith who does not do furniture, they might recommend you to a furniture dealer who does not do silver, especially if the two have an agreement each to stick to their own field.

There is one other situation, which I am quite sure would not ever involve you, where if a dealer has a real horror of a TFI, they will almost certainly recommend them to the competition and thus, at a single stroke, get rid of the TFI and confound the enemy.

It must be said, in all fairness, that there are among collectors some really great characters whose eccentricities and earthy comments completely outweigh the nausea caused by

170

the 'ugly customers', and who make the dealer's life all the more worthwhile and enjoyable. We have, over the years, given many of them nicknames. Regardless of any of this political correctness claptrap, these names are an accolade bestowed with respect and affection on those we hold dear. We know what we mean and so do they.

'Rasputin' I have already mentioned. Another was 'Young Ted' who, although he was born long after the Teddy boy era, always affected the dress of that time with the thick crepe-soled shoes, string tie and ducks-arse haircut. He would stand in the shop alternately whipping out his comb with a great flourish and resetting his DA then carefully adjusting his string tie, after which he would check his shoes and do a few dance steps. He constantly repeated this process and, at the same time, regaled us with a long, detailed and completely unintelligible report on recent events in his life. 'So, anyway, my Mabel came round but didn't stay because she had to see my other sister who really isn't but my father etc., etc.'

One day, in the middle of one of his soliloquies, in came dear old Rasputin.

' 'Ave yer got any?' and so on, through the usual procedure followed by the mandatory half a dozen bye byes when he left. At this point, Young Ted whipped out his comb and, on applying it to his DA, commented, 'Blimey, you get some funny buggers in here.' We do indeed.

Another great hero of ours was a chap who always carried a walking stick with a carved horse's head handle, hence 'Mr Horse's Head'. He would arrive bang on 11.45, go through the items that needed a bit of restoration and, after much comment and criticism, would select the ones he wanted and ask us to keep them for him as he would be back later. Sure enough, at almost exactly 2.30, he came back, paid us the money and departed.

He kept this up for years until, one day, I asked him why he always followed this same procedure. He explained that when he left us at about noon, he always went to the Dog And Duck until closing time, then back to us to collect his purchases. Now enlightened, I commented somewhat patronisingly, how very wise he was not to take his purchases into a pub, especially guns.

'No, it's not that,' he replied. 'I just can't face paying your prices until I've had a skinfull!'

It was also Mr Horse's Head who, on one occasion when the shop was full of lookers and browsers, he at one end and me at the other, cut through the intervening hubbub of inanities with the historic question, 'I say, Mr Rothery, would you be terribly offended if someone actually bought something?'

One of my nicest customers who has been with me for years and knows the house rules well, shocked me one day when, without asking, he stretched over my desk and picked up an item which had just come in and started fiddling with it.

'Mr Eastman! I am surprised at you of all people picking things off of my desk. After all these years, you ought to know better!' I admonished him sternly.

He apologised profusely then, with a twinkle in his eye, said, 'Mr Rothery. I am surprised at you, after all your years in the trade, leaving a new and interesting item on your desk, when you know full well that the first collector to come in will immediately pick it up and start fiddling with it. It should have been put away.'

It was then my turn to apologise profusely. He was, of course, quite right. Thank you, Mr Eastman. Us dealers too need to be reminded how things should be done occasionally.

Why, oh why, do collectors run a mile when a really interesting and unique item appears? All of my career I have been amazed that so-called collectors will not show any interest in something unless they can run to a book and identify it. Date, maker, type etc., etc.

Surely if an object is of great age, beautiful and interesting, and is so rare that nobody has a picture or information on it, then it must be all the more collectable? Am I alone in this belief or is there some other free-thinking spirit out there? Ok, I know I keep telling you that I'm not a collector, but if I was this is the field that would interest me. I have absolutely no wish to own a piece of china identical to thousands of others. I will not be told by a book that an item doesn't exist when I'm sitting here holding it in my hand. Here's a thought when you've got a mystery. Do you really want to find out all about an item or is it more fun to speculate as to how it came about and why?

It is alleged that I'm some sort of expert on firearms – not a theory that I subscribe to, but it brings in a lot of well-paid consultancy work and my clients appear happy. So imagine, if you will, there I was sitting in this modest house, looking at what is obviously a real, working, superbly made P 08 pistol (Luger to you). Not a mark on it – no maker, no number, no proof marks – absolutely nothing. The old gent who had called me sat opposite with a twinkle in his eye. 'You're the gun expert. What do you make of that?'

One thing I learnt years ago is don't try to bullshit old gentlemen who probably know more than you do. What a pity young collectors do not learn that these days.

'The truth is I don't know, sir. It's obviously what is incorrectly called a Luger pistol. It's nine-millimetre calibre, superbly made, so not German general military manufacture. It could be Swiss, but they tended to use smaller calibre. This might surprise you, but I'm tempted to think it was made in England by the engineering firm of Vickers. They did make some for the Dutch. However, in the absence of any marking, I have to admit I honestly don't know.'

The old gent walked over to the sideboard and, to my amazement, returned with two glasses of whisky.

'Well done, son, you're absolutely right. But what you don't know is that I worked in the pattern room when we made the prototypes for the Dutch contract, and what nobody else knows, I made a spare one for myself and that's it.'

What a fool I was not to have kept that pistol. It was unique, not in any books, only the old boy and I knew the full story. That pistol was probably destroyed in the recent monumental act of governmental vandalism that took place after the terrible tragedy at Dunblane.

A delicate subject that must be mentioned is when there is a dispute between the dealer and the collector. Even among reasonable decent people disagreements can arise although, with care, they can be avoided in the first place. Dare I suggest that that is partially what this book is about? When a dispute results in a permanent rift, it really does nobody any good. The dealer loses a valued customer and the collector loses a reliable source of supply and guidance.

How then can we avoid such a sad state of affairs arising? Firstly, take a long hard look at the item and, if you have any misgivings, mention them to the dealer. If you still have doubts then, for goodness sake don't buy it. All too often I hear, 'I wasn't really happy when I bought it.' Well, in that case, why did the idiot buy it?

There is an old saying, 'if you have to think about it, you don't want it.' If you have a friend whose opinion you value, by all means take them along to advise you, but do remember, the dealer will not be as interested in your friend's opinion as you are.

A story that illustrates this concerns a very long-standing client of mine who I nearly lost in the old days when, having discussed an item at great length, he finally agreed to buy it. As I was about to wrap it up, he said, 'Just a minute, Mr Rothery. Before I actually take that, I will bring my friend in to check it.'

Seeing the look on my face, he asked, 'Is that a problem?'

'Well, sir, not really. But may I ask what profession your friend is?'

'Certainly. He is an accountant. Why do you ask?'

'Well, sir, I know that you are the senior partner in one of Portsmouth's oldest and most respectable law firms.'

'Mr Rothery, that is most kind of you, but what on earth has it got to do with the subject in hand?'

'Mr Smith, if I asked you to do the conveyance on one of my properties but insisted that my friend, who is a bus driver, should check to see if you had done it properly before I signed it, what might your reaction be?'

He thought for a moment then laughed, 'Good point. I'll take it with me.'

That gentleman is, after 30 years, still a highly valued client of mine because I bow to his superior knowledge of the law and he bows to mine on matters of antiques.

Try please to understand this basic concept. You are highly professional in your own field and not the slightest bit interested in the opinions of amateurs. Neither is the professional antiques dealer. Bear this in mind as we move on to the question of resolving any disputes that might arise between you and a dealer.

If, on the one hand, the guy who has upset you is not one of your regular dealers and you are not too concerned, then it doesn't matter overmuch whether you fall out with him or not. If, on the other hand, he is a regular, useful source, then the last thing you want is to fall out with him permanently. Before you go roaring in, full of righteous indignation, think. Is it worth making an issue of? You surely don't want to upset the apple cart over a few quid? If, at a later date, you mention in passing that you were a bit put out by what happened, the dealer will probably be so embarrassed that he will generously compensate you on your next purchase.

If the matter is more serious then the calm 'more hurt than angry' approach is always best. Make sure you are talking to the right person who has the authority to do something about your complaint. Tell them clearly and without embellishments exactly what your complaint is and produce the offending article together with any relevant paperwork. When you have made your case, give the person you are talking to a chance to check out the facts and listen to their side of the story without interruption. In the vast majority of cases, given goodwill and good manners on both sides, most disputes can be resolved amicably. If anyone roars into a business establishment and starts laying into a junior member of staff who has no idea what the guy is shouting about and no authority to take any action if they did know, then the whole situation becomes rather sad and silly.

Sitting one day at my desk in the old Marmion Road shop, I was suddenly confronted by a very irate gentleman accompanied by a rather large friend. My cheery 'Good morning, sir' and welcoming smile were greeted with a string of abuse and the allegation that I had sold the gentleman's wife a piece of china which was, among other things, overpriced, a poor fake and showing signs of recent repair. He further informed me that unless I gave him her money back, plus the cost of him and his pal the expert taking a day off work, he would do me great injury. During this tirade I had tried several times to interject but it was only when he finally ran out of wind that I was able to explain to him that we didn't sell china and ask him if he might possibly have the wrong shop!

If all else fails, then you might have to get some sort of independent opinion. Again, I stress that such an opinion will be worthless unless it comes from an established and respected member of the trade. Most proper dealers would accept, maybe reluctantly, such an opinion, even if it differed from their own.

God forbid, but should the matter sadly get to the courts, they will not be interested in the evidence of anyone other than a bona fide expert.

It would be a sad day indeed if nice, intelligent people like you and your dealer could not resolve any differences without recourse to any outside bodies.

11

Farewell

This is, for me, the most difficult part of the book to write. Having told you how to build and protect your much-beloved collection, we must face the fact that one day it will pass into other hands. How then, when the party is over, do we go about disposing of our treasures?

I once ran an experiment by asking my regulars this question and was most surprised at their answers. These varied from publishing a price list to advertising in the local free paper, and included the usual idea of putting the lot in auction, plus the less usual idea of taking a stall at a fair. Few had thought of consulting their friendly local dealer on the matter and several expressed surprise at the suggestion.

Let us consider the pros and cons of the saner of these various methods of disposal.

Advertising in magazines and newspapers will give your goods the maximum exposure, but will all the people who answer your ads be the sort of person you want poking about your house? Some of them will indeed be genuine collectors like yourself but you will also get the fringe dealers and chancers trying to pick up a bargain, with the risk that if they don't get one, they will come back later and help themselves.

Even the genuine collectors won't want all your goods so you stand a fair chance of still being left with the less popular items. Do not for one minute think that collectors always pay a better price than dealers. Many are the times I have bought at a house and the vendor has commented, 'I offered that to a couple of collectors who were advertising for stuff and they didn't offer me anything like the amount you have.'

You could take a stall at a fair with very similar results. Your lovely bits and pieces will be manhandled and criticised and silly offers made for them. You will still not sell them all and again will be left with some of the less popular items. The only good thing is that this ghastly experience will not take place in your home with the attendant risks to your family.

What about auction, then? Assuming you go to a proper auction house, you cut out all the hard work and most of the security risks. There are the other risks that I have outlined in the chapter on auctions. It is almost an odds-on certainty that some of your treasures will fetch prices beyond your expectations and some will be well below what you hoped for. Overall, the total will come out at about what the auctioneer estimated. You will certainly take exception to some of the descriptions of your favourite objects. There will still be some pieces that do not sell and these will have to go into the next sale or be returned to you.

Remember the auctioneers' charges. If, say, your collection makes £10,000, you will get back between £7,000 and £8,000. Remember also the time lapse in payment (from several weeks to several months) before the money is actually in your hands.

We must, of course, not forget the run-in time from when the man in the brown coat collects to the next sale or, worse still, the next specialist sale, of which there are only two a year, the next being in five months time. All in all, it could actually be as much as a year between you waving goodbye to your collection and getting the money. You should think very hard about this method of disposal, especially if you have a pressing need for your money.

'Dealers never want to give you anything,' or 'Dealers want to make a profit so they won't give you much,' and 'Dealers never want to buy anything back.' You have heard these things said and so have I. That sort of talk is absolute rubbish.

Real dealers are desperate to buy in good stock. As I have said elsewhere in this book, if they don't buy they have nothing to sell and if they don't sell they don't eat. Most proper dealers are also, you will be surprised to hear, deeply hurt and offended when their favourite, regular customer sells their collection and does not give them a chance to make an offer. There are dozens of items that I can think of that I would love to buy back, and at a lot more money than I sold them for. Indeed, on many occasions, it has been a condition of sale that the purchaser gets the object only if, should they ever want to sell it, I get first refusal. I have mentioned before that star customers get star treatment and this would most certainly include the regular getting a special price whether they are buying or selling.

Of course dealers make a profit, that is why they are in business, but it is nothing like the silly stories you see on TV. I shall not be popular in the trade for telling you this, but let me explain how real dealers operate. They do, of course, vary a bit, dependent on the person's approach to the subject.

Most have a target gross profit of, say, 50 per cent which is the ideal they look for. So an item costing £50 is marked up at £75 plus, maybe a little bit more to knock off if they play the silly haggling game. Sometimes they get lucky and are offered something for £10 which they can sell for £100. Sometimes they pay £100 and, after a long hard struggle, get fed up with the item and take a loss. At the end of the year, the 'victories' tend to equate with the 'disasters'.

Most of the business is done in the middle field. It is here that the trade sayings of 'a little profit is better than no profit' and 'you can't go bust taking a profit' come in to play. If, for the sake of argument, we have an item which will sell at £1,000, the dealer (for fear of losing it) will offer a sensible price of £600 or £700 and may go up to £800 on the basis that

£200 profit is better than nothing. A few might, by the same argument, go up to £900 and there are the odd fools who will speculate £950 to make £50, but if they do that, too often they don't tend to last long.

It should be noted that many other factors come in to consideration, such as has the dealer got two already but will accept a third if it's cheap enough, or have they got too much stock in general and the bank on their back to reduce their overdraft? In reverse, if they are desperately short of stock or can place the item straight away, then they may pay a bit more. Also, collectors tend not to believe me when I tell them this but it is perfectly true: the offer may well be affected by how much the dealer likes or dislikes the vendor.

Now then, how does all this affect the price you get for your collection?

The first thing you have learnt is that, contrary to the rubbish on TV, no reputable dealer is going to offer £100 for an item worth £1,000, not for any moral reason or because they're a nice person, but because they're terrified of losing it and the profit that goes with it.

When it comes to your stuff, Rupert from the auctioneers tells you that the collection will make about £10,000 and, after charges, you will get back about £8,000 some time in the future, plus any unsold lots. So when your tame dealer offers £7,000–£8,000 for the lot, including the less saleable items, with the added advantage of payment in full and collection tomorrow, it starts to make a lot of sense to sell to the dealer, especially if you can get them to up their offer to £8,000 rather than £7,000.

Dare I even suggest that, in view of all the help the dealer has given you over the years, it is a wonderful chance to show your appreciation in a practical manner that not only costs you nothing but might even save you a few bob? It's an old-fashioned idea called loyalty.

There is one pitfall of which people selling up a collection should be wary. Sometimes, even nice people like you fail to see the full picture. They sell the bits that their friends wanted to their buddies, then Rupert takes the more important pieces to Sleazies, leaving the dross to be sold to the local tame dealer without whose help the collection might not have been formed in the first place. They are then surprised when Mr Nice Guy makes them a derisory offer or suggests they dispose of their rubbish in a painful and physically impossible way.

Whether you are giving up the collection or not, be warned: should you have the misfortune to come into contact with auctioneers, among their many nasty tricks is a tendency to take the decent items and tell the vendor that the rubbish could be better sold to the local dealers. In other words, they don't want it. They then cause the vendor untold embarrassment by suggesting ludicrously high values for this same rubbish that they don't want. The result is that the poor vendor gets laughed out of every shop in the area with the advice, 'Well, if Sleazies told you it was worth that, let the idiots buy it.'

One method of disposing of anything that I most strongly advise you against is leaving items with a dealer on sale or return – i.e., selling an object or collection on commission. It rarely works for a number of reasons. Firstly, the dealer is obviously going to sell their own stock first because there is a proper profit in it as opposed to a bit of commission on your item. The problem of part-exchanges then raises its ugly head. You see that your item has gone from the shelf and quite reasonably expect your money, only to be told that the dealer has had to take a part-exchange and you will have to wait for *that* item to sell before getting your money. If the item fails to sell and, when you go to collect it, you notice a bit of damage that you feel sure was not there when you took it in, more arguments arise.

About 50 per cent of disputes on which I am asked to arbitrate concern sale or return or goods left for sale on commission. Most dealers will not even contemplate this sort of arrangement but others, usually those with little or no capital, welcome it. This is probably why, on so many occasions, when the owner goes to collect their goods or money, they find the shop closed and the dealer gone.

There it is. The choice is yours. Let me point out, however, should anyone challenge what I have said and suggest that my advice is such because I am a dealer and want to buy these things for myself, that before this book is published I shall have retired and be living in France and therefore have no axe to grind.

Let us suppose that rather than break up your collection, you are contemplating passing it on in its entirety. If you have a relative who is as keen as you are and is going to love and care for it, perhaps even continue and build it up further, that is a wonderful situation. It is also rather a rare situation. Sadly, it is more common for a collector to find that nobody in the family is in the slightest bit interested.

I often have one or other of my clients say to me, 'Mr Rothery, you know I have always told you that I was building up my collection to leave to the kids? Well, none of them is interested. How do you suggest I dispose of it?'

Again, they express surprise when I tell them, 'Well, sir, I would love to buy it.'

In all fairness, I suppose that some members of the family, especially the youngsters, may not have the same love for a collection that you and I have and might well prefer a computer.

The really ugly side of this sort of situation is when, as soon as the son, daughter or nephew gets their greedy little hands on it, they rush straight out and flog the old man's lifetime collection to the nearest dealer. I have actually been in the lounge, with the poor old boy in his coffin, while the grieving widow has sold me his collection off the wall and used the coffin top as a table to do so.

One event that has always given me great joy was when one

of my best-loved clients of many years standing said to me one day, 'What do you think my collection is worth?' Knowing the gentleman to be of some substance and in no need to sell his collection, I assumed the question was purely rhetorical and jokingly said, 'More than I've got in the float. You will have to take a rather large cheque.' To my surprise, he assured me that he was serious. So I worked out a price which he agreed was about what he had expected and told me he would be in with the collection the next Friday. Would I please ensure that someone was available to help him unload and would I also ensure that payment would be in cash?

The following Friday, after the transaction had been completed, but before I gave him the money, I asked him, 'Look, sir, are you absolutely sure about this? I really do not want your family descending on me at a later date and accusing me of diddling them out of their inheritance.'

He sat down and, leaning on the desk, explained to me, 'You see, Mr Rothery, whenever members of my family gather at my house, they have great arguments and discussions as to the disposal of my collection. Who is going to have what or should the collection be sold and the money split between them etc., etc? They do not see fit to include me in these debates or to enquire as to what my wishes might be in the matter. Indeed, they completely ignore my presence. I have therefore decided to sell you the collection and for you to pay me cash so that I may go up to my club and treat myself and my old chums to one last, glorious binge, which will last until the money runs out.'

He stood up and, shaking my hand, said, 'Mr Rothery, over the years you have shown me many kindnesses and done me many services. I have no doubt whatsoever that my family will make enquiries of you as to what happened to my collection. When that time comes, Mr Rothery, will you please do me one final service and tell them what I have done and why?'

I squeezed his hand more firmly and, looking him in the

eye, told him, 'Sir, it will be my honour and my pleasure to do so.'

Perhaps you have thought of giving/leaving your collection to a museum? If your collection is of great local, national or international importance and you are in a position to also provide the funds to house and maintain it, I can only admire and applaud your generosity and public spirit. If it is a good, average or better than average collection, and even if you can afford to give away hundreds or thousands of pounds, please don't. It is true that such is the boundless rapacity of the average museum curator, that they will accept it and probably send you a letter of thanks but, in all likelihood, it will be consigned to the cellars and never see daylight again. I have mentioned earlier in this book that only about 10 per cent of the stuff in museums is ever on show.

When, in the late 1700s, the will of a French aristocrat and antiques collector was published, his instructions for the disposal of his collection were detailed and precise. The collection was to be scattered for sale over as great a part of Europe as possible and under no circumstances was any part of it to end up in the hands of a museum. In a codicil to the will, he explained that for years he had had the sheer joy of seeking out the items and loving and caring for them during his stewardship of them. Rather than have them consigned to the dusty cellar of a museum, he wanted them made available to as wide a spectrum of fellow collectors and future generations of collectors as possible, so that they too could share the pleasure that he had enjoyed from them. I don't know his name but he was a true collector and the rest of us would not go far wrong in taking a leaf out of his book.

Honestly, I am not paranoid about little old ladies but they are constantly cropping up whatever subject is under discussion. In this case, it is the monotonous regularity with which they appear clutching an object and explaining that 'he' always wanted it to go to the museum. When you tell them it's worth a couple of hundred pounds then, regardless of what 'he' wanted, they sell it to you. If you tell them it has no value, the usual answer is, 'Well, if it's not worth anything, I'll present it to the museum.'

An odd situation occasionally arises when one of my departed collectors makes me executor of their collection or leaves other instructions that its disposal is to be left to Mr Rothery. This invariably involves a lot of hard work as I feel an obligation to do my very best for them, sometimes working harder than I do on my own stock. No gentleman would, of course, look for any financial remuneration for meeting this sacred trust, the end result being lots of additional hard work and no payment. But I'll tell you what, it really is a great compliment.

As I said at the beginning of this chapter, disposing of a collection is not a subject that we like to think about but we all must. I do so hope that my comments are of some use to you and trust that it may be many years before you need to consider my advice.

This is not the end.
It is not even the beginning of the end.
But it is, perhaps, the end of the beginning.

Winston Churchill